From Percy to Peter

A History of Dyslexia

Jenni Beard

≋ WATERSIDE PRESS

From Percy to Peter: A History of Dyslexia
Jenni Beard

ISBN 978-1-909976-67-2 (Paperback)
ISBN 978-1-910979-79-2 (Epub ebook)
ISBN 978-1-910979-80-8 (Adobe ebook)

Cover design © 2019 Waterside Press by www.gibgob.com with assistance from Esther North.

Printed and bound Severn, Gloucester, UK.

Main UK distributor Gardners Books, 1 Whittle Drive, Eastbourne, East Sussex, BN23 6QH. Tel: +44 (0)1323 521777; sales@gardners.com; www.gardners.com

North American distribution Ingram Book Company, One Ingram Blvd, La Vergne, TN 37086, USA. Tel: (+1) 615 793 5000; inquiry@ingramcontent.com

Cataloguing-In-Publication Data A catalogue record for this book can be obtained from the British Library.

Ebook *From Percy to Peter: A History of Dyslexia* is available as an ebook and also to subscribers of Ebrary, Ebsco, Myilibrary and Dawsonera.

Published 2019 by
Waterside Press Ltd.
Sherfield Gables, Sherfield on Loddon,
Hook, Hampshire, RG27 0JG.

Online catalogue WatersidePress.co.uk

Table of Contents

About the author

Jenni Beard went to school in Surrey and Sussex. Her higher education took place at Whitelands College of Education, where she obtained her teaching certificate and Goldmiths, University of London, where she completed a diploma course in textile design. She undertook the British Dyslexia Association Diploma Course for teaching those with Specific Learning Difficulties (Dyslexia) before obtaining an MA in Biography at Buckingham University.

She has worked as an infants teacher, playgroup leader, night school teacher, textile technician, technical tutor, supply teacher, secondary school special needs teacher and university support adviser.

A mother of three and grandmother of four she is a gardener, knitter and lover of dogs.

Jenni Beard did not discover that she was dyslexic until her son Peter was diagnosed with the condition following which she came to realise that she too was affected by it, though it took some years after that for her to undergo a formal assessment.

Acknowledgements

So many people have helped me on this journey that I am bound to miss some out and to them my apologies.

David McLoughlin and the British Dyslexia Association for starting me on this course of study and thought.

The Buckingham University Biography Group and particularly Professor Jane Ridley for the tools and inspiration to write this work.

The pioneers of the dyslexic movement, Tim Miles, Sandhya Naidoo, Gill Cotterell, Helen Arkell and Bevè Hornsby who were kind enough to talk to me but also to all of those I met through their writings.

Davison School, Worthing for the giving me the courage to become a teacher.

Lastly, but of course not least, my wonderful children: Charlotte, Esther and Peter and my oldest friends and supporters Anthea Chambers and Penny Guy.

In memory of Robert John Beard 1947–2018,
husband, supporter and best friend.

Introduction

Word-blind, what can this mean? Not being able to see words, ignoring them, turning a blind-eye? Word-blind was the term used at the turn of the twentieth century and for many decades to describe dyslexic people. Many other terms were used to describe the condition, including dyslexia itself, but the group of people who came together at the beginning of the 1960s to act for dyslexic people decided to adopt the term word-blind and called their research and teaching unit the Word Blind Centre.

Discovering that you are dyslexic is an odd experience, a mixture of relief and irritation. All the little methods you have of remembering and organizing your life seem normal to you and you think this is the way everyone functions, but to find this is not so is isolating. Understanding that you are dyslexic may take years and for many adults this realisation may be the result of first discovering that their child has the condition. Undertaking an assessment resolves the question "Am I dyslexic or just thick?"

If you do take the plunge and get yourself assessed and discover, yes, you do have the condition there is relief but also anger. Knowledge does help you to understand why childhood was difficult and why it took years to come out of the "pea soup" that is a dyslexic child's world but there is also a welter of "if onlys" to contend with. This book is mainly about children and luckily more of them are recognised as being dyslexic at an early age and for them I hope life is sunnier than it was before the Word Blind Centre.

This book is an attempt to document historically the place the dyslexic child has found within education. The Dyslexia Institute wisely recommends that a teacher of dyslexics has taught the average child before he or she can recognise the odd educational mixture that is the dyslexic child. Note "average" not "normal" because, as taught in the 1960s, there is no such animal as the latter; each child is an individual and will have his or her own strengths and weaknesses.

The dyslexia movement has sought to show that dyslexic people have a pattern of difficulties that are different to the average child but that they can be helped by basic good teaching. To view the dyslexic child we need to see where he or she fits within the history of education. The first *documented* account of a dyslexic child was in 1896 with a boy called Percy, but Percy can't have been the *first* dyslexic child. Prior to Percy did anyone notice such children and, if they did, did they care? What schools were available, what literature was there to read, who was taught to read and write and who were the teachers?

All the works on dyslexia mention Percy but few go into detail about the research into non-readers between 1896 and the Word Blind Centre which started in the early-1960s. However, there was a lot of work on the subject; it just didn't come under the title of word-blind or dyslexia and it takes a little imagination to realise that often the researchers were looking at dyslexic children as well as other non-readers. Alfred White Franklin was to pull together the many threads that made up the research into the word-blind and as a result, through the Invalid Children's Aid Association (ICAA), called a conference in 1961 to look into the subject of dyslexia then called word-blindness.

This is jumping ahead, because to understand why Percy's parents and teachers were worried about his non-reading it is necessary to look at schools in the late-Victorian period and how schooling progressed from that of the mainly religious-based establishments of the middle-ages to the huge institutions seen at the end of the nineteenth century. The researchers looking at non-reading children and how to teach them require a chapter of their own as do the people who were active in the dyslexia movement in the 1960s and beyond: see *The Pioneers* (*Chapter Six*). This brings us to the stormy 1961 conference (*Chapter Four*).

The *Word Blind Centre* (*Chapter Six*) is at the heart of this work but it was necessary to divert a little into some of the norms and pressures of the time which gave me *Chapter Five, Class, Madness and Charities* and another side-step into parents, friends and pupils. The concluding chapters review the work undertaken by the Word Blind Centre and what has come out of it. *Chapter Nine* asks *What Happened Next?* Currently dyslexia still appears periodically in the news and experts are still arguing, so there is no definite conclusion (my own thoughts towards the end this book must be seen in this light).

This book is also a group biography looking at not just at the syndrome dyslexia but the people who worked in the field, the detractors, and the physical space at Coram's Fields that was the Word Blind Centre. Hopefully, those involved, be they dyslexics, parents or educators will feel less isolated when they see how old is the struggle and how worthwhile the cause. It is in no way a scientific work but references have been included by way of footnotes for those who want to look in more depth at any given aspect. With dyslexics in mind it is possible to read the chapters separately, to change the order or leave chunks out completely.

The beginnings

So to begin with, in November 1896, an article by Dr W Pringle Morgan entitled "A Case of Congenital Word-blindness" appeared in the *British Medical Journal.*[1] This initiated the research into dyslexia and all the arguments that were to follow. In it he described a 14-year-old boy "Percy F", who could not read. Percy was a clever boy, a teenager he would be called nowadays. Pringle Morgan writes of Percy's abilities in many subjects and his particular aptitude in arithmetic, but only when taught *orally.* One of his teachers who had worked with him for years reckoned he was the brightest boy in the school if he was only taught in that way. However Percy could not read, he had been at school for seven years and although he recognised the alphabet and a few small words that was it, and his teachers were at a loss to understand why.

Although the article was the first to record a case of a child with "word-blindness", the doctor was familiar with the condition, later writing "cases of wordblindness are always interesting". Those Pringle Morgan had come across before were in conjunction with damage to the brain through injury or illness, but his eyes had been opened to a connection

---

1.   *British Medical Journal*, 1896, 2, p. 1387.

with the likes of Percy through another article, this time in *The Lancet* by James Hinshelwood, an ophthalmologist.[2] Pringle Morgan reported:

> "It was your paper — may I call it your classical paper? — on wordblindness and visual memory published ... on December 21st, 1895, which first drew my attention to this subject, and my reason for publishing this case was that there was no reference anywhere, so far as I knew to the possibility of the condition being congenital."

What amazed the medical people was that this otherwise healthy child, Percy, was showing the same symptoms, i.e. not being able to read, which were normally only seen in some stroke victims or the brain injured.[3] A group of medics were beginning to think that there was a possibility a group of children was born with the disorder hence use of the word "congenital".

Pringle Morgan was medical officer to one or more of Seaford's many preparatory schools and it was at one of these that he met Percy who in 1896 would normally have been about to move to secondary school.[4] Poor old Percy, no more is heard of him, but he had managed to learn his letters, was bright and had parents and teachers who cared for him, so hopefully he prospered.

---

2.   Hinshelwood, J, "Word-blindness and Visual Memory", *The Lancet*, 1895, Vol. 2, p. 1564.
3.   Later as we will see part of the test for dyslexia was a questionnaire for a child's parents where questions on possible birth injuries were posed.
4.   Although education was now compulsory in the UK, children did not automatically go on to secondary school. Percy was being educated within the private sector so it would have been more than likely that he moved to secondary education.

CHAPTER ONE

Questions

The story begins in 1896 with changes for Percy but this was also a time of change for education in England and Wales generally. The year 1870 saw William Forster's Elementary Education Act[1] which was to bring education to all. In the 1860s, £800,000 was provided by government to church schools but there was growing pressure for non-denominational schools also to be funded by the state. Industrialists were pushing to have the country's youth educated as, due to the lack of universal education, Britain was falling behind other European countries particularly Germany. The funding for church schools remained and school boards were established to administer non-denominational schools.[2] It took until 1880 for education to be compulsory following the Royal Commission on the Factory Acts, which recommended that it be made compulsory in order to stop child labour.

For Percy, a child from a middle-class family, not to being able to read would have been an embarrassment as well as an inconvenience; it was becoming unacceptable not to be reading. Compulsory education was not free until 1891 however. The 1870 Act merely stated that all children should be educated from the age of five to ten years.

Until the 1960s education was never about the child as an individual, child education was concerned with the needs of society, commerce and religion. The 1960s saw the child beginning to take centre stage. Forms of communication, whether pictorial, hieroglyphics or written are as old as history but those who could read the images fell into two groups: those

---

1. A statue of William Forster stands in Embankment Gardens just near Charing Cross Railway Station as he looks seriously across the River Thames.
2. The term "board school" comes from the setting-up of educational boards.

who read for pleasure or as scholars and those who read for others, and both groups may have learnt reading skills as children. The Romans have left evidence of this; they used carved ivory letters to help children read.

Reading is a complicated and difficult process. Try dissecting the different stages, it brings home just how clever the brain is to hold each action and thought and add them together to form a word which in turn becomes a concept or idea. Man must have had a need to record his thoughts and actions so that he could later remember them or felt he wanted to pass ideas and events on to others; cave paintings and carved objects are the earliest evidence of this. This way of recording has continued but writing was a shorthand method of communicating.

English is a particularly complicated language made up as it is from different language roots and somehow the reader of English has to interpret the 26 letters that make up the alphabet. Each of these has a name and a sound and they can be read as single letters or in pairs and groups (blends) which alter according to where vowels are placed amongst consonants. The permutations are almost endless.

The Romans used the written word more as an aid to memory and they spoke Latin but wrote in Greek. Today's youngsters would have enjoyed the graffiti the Roman's went in for, examples of which still exist on the walls of Pompei. Words, grammar and regularised spelling are a relatively modern concept; originally sounds, letters, were written down and the reader interpreted the sounds into words by reading aloud. This method of reading continued into the ninth century and the process of mumbling or chanting the sound of the words was commonly heard in the scriptorium (described on page 15). This has been likened to the way young Muslim scholars memorise the Koran today.

Although man has found the need to record information be it historical events or rules only a few people could interpret these writings and in Western culture those interpreters were usually but not exclusively in religious houses. The readers must have been so clever they could organize the symbols into a meaning and interpret these ideas which were not even in their spoken language. Reading took place aloud, letters were strung together and the reader would group the sounds into words; as the practice of silent reading grew, making reading faster, this left no time to organize the sounds. Words were a necessity and grammar was needed to make sense for the average reader. In the first half of the fifteenth century there was some organization in the structure as the differences from one book to another added to the confusion. A standard style was developed (*lettre bâtarde*) borrowing punctuation from Latin and using capital letters and paragraphs, all to make it easier for those less familiar with reading to comprehend.

Books were rare of course, hand written on vellum in Britain, and took years to make. The creation of these amazing objects usually took place in monasteries and the scriptorium was the lightest and warmest room or area in the monastery. Presumably odd notes were written on less important surfaces like the clay and wax blocks such as have been found in archaeological digs.

To be able to read and write was not therefore the norm and most people who could read were of high rank, but this was not always the case. Young men and boys have always been taught to write and sometimes read to serve the authorities. Schools as we would understand them can be dated back to the middle of the first millennia. Canterbury, Rochester and York's religious houses had schools and boys were trained to write, read and sing, all for the glory of God. In actual fact teaching these scribes was nearer to a training ground for civil servants than to be religious. Society, until the Reformation, was administered by centres based around religious houses. Welfare, health, education and the rule of law were administered by the religious and the funds usually came from noble families. When Henry VIII and later his son Edward VI dissolved the monasteries many of the schools continued, usually called grammar schools, coming from the teaching of grammar. The most notable public schools of the twenty-first century started life this way and ironically were for the education of poor but bright boys. Rich men also set up schools and or paid for scholars so that they had a supply of literate scribes and clerks to look after their businesses. These patrons were often nobles but in time wealthy farmers and merchants also saw the benefit of employing men who could administer funds and holdings. There was no need to read if you had someone who could do it for you. Notable among these scribes were Thomas Wolsey later to be

Cardinal Wolsey who was the son of a butcher and Thomas Cromwell later Chancellor of England who was the son of a blacksmith.

An early example of law and literacy coming together was the construction of the *Doomsday Book* in 1086. William the Conqueror commissioned the work and it covered most of England and noted everything about the country, the number of people, what was produced and who did what. It was written mainly in Latin using English words when there was no usable translation. Needless to say it was used to tax the English as William saw rich England as a cash cow but it was also for political control. William never saw the work, as by the time it was completed he was back in Normandy. There were two books: large and small. The larger volume was probably made by one scribe in one year and was particular to England and no equivalent work has been found anywhere else in Europe.

The percentage of the population who were literate began to change with the invention of the printing press which also coincided with changes in attitudes to Christian religion in Europe. Even after the Reformation, although England and Wales had moved away from the authority of the Pope, basic understanding of Christianity was still Catholic and the scriptures were interpreted by the religious. Scholars and the nobility read and there were other books such as romantic legends and even comic books but the general population relied on the clergy to interpret the bible for them and on storytellers for entertainment. Medieval church walls were covered in colourful often violent murals depicting the stories of the bible for the priest to use as visual aids to teach the consequences of not abiding by the laws of the church. In Northern Europe this was changing and Protestants read and interpreted religious texts for themselves.

In Germany in the fifteenth century Gutenberg invented the printing press making the ownership of books possible for many more of the population. In England the reading of these new printed bibles was still frowned on and Henry VIII treated those caught with copies extremely harshly, but to no avail. The genie was out of the bottle, books continued to appear, were copied by hand, and the new interpretation of Christianity continued covertly until, under Queen Elizabeth 1, Protestantism became the state religion.

William Caxton (1422–1492) born in Kent was to set up the first English printing presses in Westminster in 1467. He was apprenticed to a merchant in Holland at the age of 16, gained an education, and was encouraged by Margaret Duchess of Burgundy to translate "The Recuyell of the Histories of Troye" from French into English. In the early-1470s he lived in Cologne and there learnt how to print. So books were being read more universally and although mainly in Latin they were also being written in the vernacular (the language of an area). Chaucer's *Canterbury Tales* was one of the first books written in English and it was also one of the first to be printed by Caxton. The early printers Caxton and Richard Pynson are held responsible for the beginning of standardisation of English grammar as they had to make sense of handwritten proofs; this is probably not strictly true but is a nice story. The regularising of spelling however took much longer. Samuel Johnson's *A Dictionary of the English Language* sees a standardised language in 1755.[3]

The advent of the printing press also saw the beginning of newspapers. The majority of the population still relied on the town crier for news but between 1640 and the Restoration there were many thousands of newsletters and newspapers in existence and in 1702 the first daily newspaper the *Daily Courant* was published.[4]

To be able to read the would-be reader has to be able to see a symbol and know what it sounds like. If the sounds make up a simple visual word a picture can be used to aid the reader, so c a t = cat and the picture of the cat does the trick. But of course most sound groups don't have a picture as an aid and the reader has to learn the sounds, the images, the meaning or linkage. To complicate matters, in English the sounds don't always sound the same as they look. However difficult this reading thing is the majority of children and adults manage to learn and often with little or no effort. But not dyslexics. They have to find methods of cementing the sound, image, meaning circle in their brains and this always takes

---

3. Published on 15 April 1755 and written by Samuel Johnson, *A Dictionary of the English Language*, sometimes published as *Johnson's Dictionary*, is among the most influential dictionaries in the history of the English language.
4. Britain's press can trace its history back more than 300 years, to the time of William of Orange. Berrow's *Worcester Journal*, which started life as the *Worcester Postman* in 1690 and was published regularly from 1709, is believed to be the oldest surviving English newspaper. See also www. newspapersoc.org.uk/history-of-british-newspapers.

longer than normal. Some of the most severely dyslexic never manage to learn to read. Many dyslexics do but they tend to be slower readers and may continue to make mistakes, misunderstanding what they have read.

Historically not all of the population would have been given the opportunity to read but by the end of the seventeenth century a surprising number had some level of literacy. Like now it depended on where you lived or more likely who was in charge of your area. Boys were more likely to read than girls though many women read at home under the radar and would have taught their children including their girls. It would not have been important if you couldn't read and if anything having someone reading for you was probably seen as a status symbol. There must have always been dyslexics as dyslexia is a dominant gene and if it had caused social problems dyslexics would have been bred out of the population. Dyslexics are known for being good problem solvers and historically this must have been a greater asset than reading.

Writing was a different matter and was not always taught at the same time as reading. Into the eighteenth century it was still seen as divisive for some sections of the community to be able to write and again women were less likely to write than men, though it is highly likely that women taught themselves to write at home. Letter writing falls outside of the formal learning process in the main, though the scholars in the grammar schools used letter writing as practice. There are so many collections of letters that many must have used this intimate form of communication. The Peasants' Revolt (1381) led by Wat Tyler was fired up by the sermons or letters written by John Ball. These letters were read to "the commons" the ordinary people and caused them to revolt against the poll tax.

Paper was valuable, so letters were written for business transactions, news and affectionate messages were only added at the end of a letter. Status was important in letter writing and the higher the rank the more paper could be wasted, so letters written by Queen Elizabeth I for example show her extravagant signature surrounded by space to show how important she was. It wasn't necessary to be able to write a letter as there were always those "likely lads" who had learnt the skill and would do so for a small fee. Nothing changes of course and Martin Gilbert recounts a wonderful anecdote concerning Winston Churchill, thought to have been dyslexic, when he has a school friend write to his mother while he lies in his bath.

> "'Milbanke is writing this for me', Churchill informed his mother, 'as I am having a bath'. Milbanke was sixteen, Churchill fourteen."[5]

Before and after the 1870 Forster Act types of school varied in England and Wales. As seen, the history of schooling for the few is old, home tuition older still and with these two basic methods of teaching children the level of expertise was just as varied. The obvious person to teach a child was another family member often their mother or older sibling. If however a family member was not available, help could be brought in in the shape of governesses and tutors. Aristocrats have always had governesses and tutors. This is known from accounts of the day and literature. For example Katherine Swineford (born 1350) the mistress and later wife of John of Gaunt (whose own children were the predecessors of many of today's aristocratic and royal families) was originally a governess to his children by his first wife.[6] Governesses moved between aristocratic families and were respected members of a household.

The Industrial Revolution saw a change in the old hierarchy and the newly rich wished to progress socially. This fundamentally affected how children were taught. It became beneath a mother's (or other family member's) social standing to teach their own children and so a governess was employed to undertake their education. A governess could be a poor family member who needed a home or the daughter of a poor but educated person, for example a clergyman, and these women were well-educated but may or may not have been good teachers. As the call for governesses grew so did the number of young women with some but not necessarily much education who considered that they could fulfil the role, and saw being a governess as a way out of the working-class. Many were not well-educated but the expectation was to prepare the daughters of the house for a good marriage. That entailed the governess

---

5.   Martin Gilbert, *In Search of Churchill*, 1995, HarperCollins, p. 153.
6.   Alison Weir, *Katherine Swineford: The Story of John of Gaunt and His Scandalous Duchess*, 2007, Jonathan Cape.

in being able to play some tunes on the piano, sing, draw and speak a few words of a foreign language but not necessarily to teach their charges good basic literacy and numeracy skills.

So where did this leave the dyslexic child? In the best-case scenario, in the best place that was possible. Within the home he or she was likely to be understood, not least by other dyslexic members of the family, and with an instinctive teacher using good teaching methods and working at a rate that suited the child nothing could have been better. However governesses and tutors were also subjected to outside influences. Older boys were usually being prepared by their tutors to enter public schools and the syllabus of a school would dictate the lessons undertaken in the home schoolroom.

Tutors in the main used their position in a household to better themselves so were not necessarily sympathetic to their charges and they were bound by a classic syllabus which suited the public schools. Industrialists, the new affluent middle-class, were often from non-conformist backgrounds and the schools they set up were excellent and originally interested in mathematics and sciences but with time these also drifted towards the gentlemanly classic syllabus. It is difficult to know if either type of school would have suited the dyslexic, most likely that depended on the child and the teachers.

Governesses were in a different position but one that was no happier. There were of course splendid examples of good governesses but it is unlikely that many male or female dyslexics received the balanced well-grounded teaching they needed. It is probable that similarity to other family members, "Oh he is just like Uncle John", made the lack of reading and writing skills easy to explain away and not tackle.

Children have always been sent away from home to be educated. Education in this context must be seen in a wide context. They were placed in other families to learn a trade, as political pawns, sometimes even as hostages. With luck part of the preparation for adulthood was also learning to read, possibly to write and sometimes to calculate. Learning was not necessarily regular and would always fit the trade or the station in the social hierarchy. In medieval times it was customary for high ranking families to exchange boys and part of their education as well as learning to fight may have been academic. Boys were also apprenticed to learn a trade and literacy would be taught if it was a necessary part of the trade, Sheffield's cutlers did not pay for their boys to learn to write as their hands would probably be damaged by their trade! Boarding schools were a continuation of this process and were as diverse as society. The original charity schools metamorphosed into public schools educating the upper and the upper middle-classes.

By the eighteenth and nineteenth centuries there was also a plethora of schools which would now be termed private, they were of course fee paying but then so was most other education. These schools could and were set up by anyone and could be as small as a few children being taught by the local clergyman in his kitchen. Examples of these eighteenth and nineteenth century schools crop up in literature all the time. Jane Austen's father ran a small boys school. Girls' schools were an extension of the governess system and were often run by ex-governesses and taught the skills required to be a lady. As having some knowledge of a language was a plus these establishments were often abroad, in France, Germany and Switzerland.

There were also free boarding schools but these were definitely for the lower working-class, foundling schools and workhouse schools. These were both for the poorest in the community and not just seen as philanthropic but to guard against the moral corruption feared to be brought about by the undeserving poor. Women who became pregnant out of wedlock fell into this category and they rather than the fathers were blamed for their children. Unbelievably it was quite difficult to have your child accepted by the foundling hospitals, but if the baby was accepted the child was given a good if strict education. Similarly those children who found themselves in the workhouse were also educated. Unlike in the foundling schools there was contact with the families sometimes on a daily basis though more likely weekly. In 1839, half the inmates of workhouses were under 16 and these children were given three hours teaching a day. Some unions[7] were not happy with the high level of education given to the children of the workhouses but the sensible aim

---

7.   The 1834 Poor Law set up the Poor Law Commissioners, a central body organizing the workhouses. The day-to-day running was undertaken by groups of parishes called poor law unions.

was to train these children to be useful members of society who would in time not need to be in the workhouse. The children's wards or houses were separate from the main workhouse and in some cases these buildings were developed into industrial schools.

The industrial schools were set up in the second half of the nineteenth century and educated both boys and girls. They were written about at length in the 1904 London School Board Report. They served children of inadequate parents, or those on the edge of an illegal lifestyle and who for that reason were placed in boarding schools a distance from their homes. The children had to work hard; the regime was strict and consisted of: education, life skills, outdoor activities and nutritious food. The policy was "the devil makes work for idle hands"; the children responded to the good food, clean air and discipline. They also left school a year later than normal and were much sought after by employers so they often had jobs lined up before they left school. The girls trained as maids, teachers and needlewomen and boys often entered the army as drummer-boys as most of these schools had brass bands. The policy may have been draconian but on the surface it sounds a good working model for vagrant street children that roamed the big cities, starving and thieving.[8] Today it is reckoned that 40 per cent of boys in youth custody and prison are dyslexic. If dyslexics were sent to the industrial schools they may have fared well, the basic repetitive education and an insistence on keeping busy through organized games may well have suited them.

The Second World War saw another type of boarding school brought about as an offshoot of the child evacuation process. It was realised that not all children were best served by being sent to live with a family and these children were sent to camps. For some children this made a huge difference to their lives as they were secure and although the teaching was strict it was effective being carried out by old, usually retired, but experienced teachers. Parents were asked to contribute to the child's expenses and it was not an enforced situation like the industrial schools.

---

8.   My father lived above his parent's coffee shop on Upper Thames Street, London. In *The London School Board Report*, to my amazement, there was a "hang out" for children in an Upper Thames Street coffee house, "George's", alias the "House of Lords" where a room was set apart for their accommodation (p. 227). My father's name was the same as his father: George Henry.

The majority of children have always been taught in day schools and the different types of schools grew as the centuries progressed. In the eighteenth century when the number of people reading flourished there was little or no control over schools. The Industrial Revolution saw huge social change in England. The old aristocracy were still at the top of the class tree but the new rich industrialists were coming up close behind. Following them were the professionals, well-educated and with social standing and servicing all these groups was the new working-class aristocracy. The latter group was huge and made up of those who were "in service", or in the service industries, e.g. barbers, tradesmen, craft workers, army personnel. They numbered 25 per cent of urban population. These groups both the new middle-class and the working-class aristocracy made use of the private and public schools but this left huge numbers of children who by the turn of the nineteenth century were a worry. The authorities realised that these children had to be taught, the French Revolution had scared them.

The late-eighteenth century was a "golden time" for reading. By the seventeenth century a surprising number of people could read 60 per cent of the general population, and of these, unsurprisingly, more were men than women. However, although 60 per cent could read, far fewer could write. It is not clear as to how literate the readers were as the test of literacy was to be able to sign the wedding certificate and it is possible more people, especially women, could write as writing was seen as bucking the establishment so was frowned on even as late as the eighteenth century.

Literacy went hand in hand with the amount of time spent working, so those working on the land used all daylight hours in employment. If the rural worker had the cost of candles, the light was more likely to be used for mending and sewing than reading. The rural and urban poor had a limited knowledge of reading and recognised rather than read items using their limited skill to read stock lists and instructions. Reading was rarely just for pleasure and as a result the vocabulary of the poorest class was limited. Oral storytelling, a much-loved entertainment, was common in England well into the nineteenth century; people were good at listening and happy to be read to by an authority figure such as their father or teacher and some researchers argue that this trend slowed down literacy amongst the lower classes. Newspapers were read out loud in public houses and Charles Dickens' serialised novels were commonly read aloud in the home by a literate family member.

Although the rural poor had little time to read, the working-class aristocracy had free time and spare money. This group, because of their expertise, put pressure on the upper-classes and the newly emerging middle-class. Class pressure appears again and again in the story of dyslexia and as more ordinary people learnt to read (and read for pleasure as well as for information) so it became important to be seen to be a reader. The working-class aristocracy used their spare time to read. German travellers in the early-eighteenth century wrote of seeing British roof-tilers having newspapers passed to them during their meal breaks, and in Paris everyone was reading and always had a book in their pocket. In Britain, men and women were excited by the happenings across the channel; the French Revolution slogan "freedom, equality and fraternity" encouraged more ordinary people to learn to read. The groups affected were not the rural poor but those with time, light to read at night and a small budget to borrow books from the lending libraries and buy newspapers. The reading trend was seen in England as early as 1740. Britain and France led this revolution in reading but by 1796 the tendency had spread to Germany and was referred to as a "reading epidemic".[9]

By 1779 the authorities were scared of mounting revolutionary movements and were spurred on to improve education of the masses as in the schools children's minds could be influenced and they could be taught to conform. Monitorial schools, national schools, infant schools and evening classes were employed to instil religious values and socially acceptable behaviour. Similarly, books, magazines, newspapers and religious tracts became universally available. During the French Revolution the growing popularity of newspapers gathered momentum, as did the production of cheap pamphlets, e.g. Paine's *Rights of Man*. Although these pamphlets and newspapers were still out of the reach of the poorest people second-hand papers were circulated through libraries, coffee shops and

---

9.   Reinhard Wittman, "Was there a Reading Revolution at the End of the Eighteenth Century?", in Guglielmo Cavallo and Roger Chartier (eds), *A History of Reading in the West*, 2003, Polity Press.

alehouses.[10] Newspapers and magazines also benefited from the lifting of stamp duty in 1855, and the *Sheffield Daily Telegraph* started as the first penny national and the *Manchester Guardian*, the *Scotsman* and *Liverpool Post* became dailies. The lifting of stamp duty in 1855 coincided with improvements in the making of paper. We take paper-making for granted but the progress from single sheets of paper made from pulped white rags (never mind velum) through methods of bleaching the pulp to using wood pulp and making continuous rolls of paper was long and complicated. It wasn't until 1884 that large industrial paper mills were in production.

Libraries and reading societies started in France and libraries were a bit like clubs where people met, talked and even took refreshments; they were serious and academic. In England the introduction of the Public Library Act 1850 brought a change in the reading habits of the general population. Class reared its head again through the librarians who saw themselves as in charge of educational institutions akin to universities. They happily supplied their male middle-class readers with novels but feared providing this type of reading material to the lower classes and women because they saw novels as having little educational or moral content.

Added to the problem of morals was money, why should the ratepayer pay for this type of reading? The libraries set about providing their readers with lectures and technical talks intended to encourage the reading of instructive material but to no avail; the habit of reading novels continued to grow.[11] The librarians changed tack and started to introduce lectures on the finer forms of literature.[12] Predating the public libraries, the "circulating libraries" worked on a subscription basis and like the French libraries were centres for social gatherings especially for women. These libraries were responsible for buying a large proportion of the books printed and allowed women to read and encouraged the publication of

---

10. In the 1840s for the first time paper was made from wood pulp in Kent on the Medway estuary rather than using the more expensive rags.
11. The clergy or religious organizations installed libraries. Nathan Drake in 1709 in the parish church, Sheffield assembled a library and by 1753 that city had a circulating library.
12. This all sounds so comical until I remember that when I was a child the public libraries did not stock books by Enid Blyton as her stories were considered grammatically incorrect.

women authors. Mudies, W H Smith and Boot's or other private lending libraries continued well into the twentieth century and some were still operating in the 1960s. Novels were often produced as part works in Victorian England, Dickens' novels were publish in this manner, they were called triple-deckers; by producing the books in this way the publishers covered their costs as they went along. There were also "penny dreadfuls", usually Gothic horrors written with no end in mind, much like "soaps" on television today. Railway travel brought the price of reading down as Routledge saw the sense in producing stories that could be read during a train journey. Trains were so much more comfortable than horse drawn coaches, being well lit, warm and smooth in comparison.

In France there were libraries in even small towns and villages but not so in England, but by 1890, well after the Forster Act, libraries were well-established and could even be found in most workhouses and these contained not just books but newspapers and magazines as well. Though even as late as the 1800s public houses were often the only places to take daily newspapers, many hired them out at 1d[13] an hour. However the production and distribution of religious tracts through Sunday schools probably did more than anything else to reinforce the reading habit.

Our cosy notion of the welfare of the child was far from the minds of the Victorian authorities and the trend to educate the masses was egged-on by the publishing industry. They realised the number of school text books that would be needed to teach children to read and then to continue to impart information on other aspects of life, for example the workings of the British Empire. By the mid-nineteenth century there was a varied and plentiful supply of reading material and much of it affordable to buy or borrow but what of schooling for ordinary children? The church and the state realised that educating the masses was important, basically the authorities by the eighteenth century were scared of the populace and many towns saw charity schools opened using public subscription, and the non-conformist churches and the Church of England vied with each other in opening schools. In York as early as 1705, the Society for Promoting Christian Knowledge (SPCK) established

---

13.   There were 12 old pennies to the shilling, twenty shillings to the pound.

two schools in association with the archbishop, dean and chapter, and the local corporation. Sunday schools are associated with Robert Raikes but the Sunday school movement may date back as far as the sixteenth century. Raikes was a newspaper publisher whose interest led to the opening of a church-based Sunday school in Gloucester in 1780. With support from the Bishops of Chester and Salisbury, a London Society for the Establishment of Sunday Schools was established in 1785. By 1787, it was reckoned that there were 250,000 Sunday school pupils. By 1831, this had risen in England to over 1.25 million and by the mid-nineteenth century around two-thirds of all working-class children aged between five and 15 were attending Sunday school. Although the intention was to teach children religion it was necessary to teach them to read before they could read the bible.

Formal schooling or state schools (as they would be recognised in the twenty-first century) grew out of the Sunday School Movement. The popularity of these schools was due to Sunday being a non-work day. All churches, non-denominational or Church of England, vied with each other to provide free or cheap schooling. In Sheffield a Mr Proud described the teaching methods:

"The alphabet taught in sand
Single syllable cards
Sentences in the National Society Reading bk2
National Society Reading bk3, story of Joseph and his brothers
Abridged versions of the bible and Mrs Trimmer's scripture classe
The rote learning of prayers, psalms, catechism."[14]

Ragged schools were started by Victorian philanthropists who realised that really poor children could not attend school not only because they did not have the money for fees but because they were literally dressed in rags. The children were fed, dressed and taught to be human as well as to read and write, and of course there was a measure of religious teaching. Although this group also saw the poor as a section of society

14. Malcolm Mercer, *Schooling the Poorer Child: Elementary Education in Sheffield 1560–1902*, 1996, Sheffield Academic Press, p. 70.

to be feared as immoral they went about trying to change the situation through education.

In 1861 John Hollinghead wrote several articles for the *Morning Post,* he later collected these together in a book that he called *Ragged London.* It charts the different areas of London and the filth and degradation he came across. Hollinghead started his tour in Clerkenwell where he found ragged schools, national schools, evening schools and Sunday schools, which he wrote were "in full operation and well attended".[15] The clergy were often responsible for opening ragged schools. The Reverend Thornton with the help of a Mr Holland opened a school in an old distillery and named it the "George Yard Ragged School". Mr Lewis, their secretary, wrote of the terrible state of the children and of how they had to feed, cloth and house them as well as teach or they could not rest happily themselves until they had rescued the street urchins. Thornton hoped that by starting George Yard they would save the children from a life of crime. Education appears to have been secondary to their more basic needs. St George in the east managed to educate 1,000 boys, girls and infants using railway arches. Monies from the government, local subscriptions and pennies from the children supported these schools and in 1860 there were plans to enlarge the Middlesex Society's National School in Cannon Street founded in 1781. In Shoreditch another clergyman, the Reverend Trevitt, organized through the Metropolitan District Visiting Society, ragged schools, national schools, infant schools and Sunday schools. As in other London areas Trevitt also fed the children. The Reverend Maguire in Clarkenwell combined the ragged school with the Temperance Society.

Clothing was often distributed on Sundays and a Miss Agar recounted a conversation between a teacher and a little girl where the teacher asked the child if she would like some socks and she answered that she was well-off for socks. On enquiring how many pairs she had the child explained just the pair she was wearing and that was enough. Children or their parents were expected to contribute financially to their education but free evening classes for older children and adults were also run through

---

15.   John Hollingshead, *Ragged London in 1861*, 1861, Smith, Elder & Co, London (Elibron Classics Replica Edition unabridged).

the Sunday schools movement. All areas of London had ragged schools, national schools, infant schools and Sunday schools and educated thousands of children. The infant schools often acted as baby-minders saving children from harm but many children were still left with no education. Hollinghead wrote of London but the picture was the same in all other major industrial conurbations.

It is impossible to tell if dyslexic children learnt in the city schools, the structure and repetition would have been a good grounding but it is unlikely that a few spare pennies were spent on these children. Their country cousins may have fared better as the classes were smaller and the children better known to their teachers.

By 1813 schools for the working-classes were becoming larger and it was necessary to teach huge numbers and monitorial schools were developed after the French model to cope with this situation. These schools had masters and monitors, the latter chosen from the oldest children. The master was usually the headteacher and he put together a programme which the monitors administered. The lessons were simple and designed to give children the basics known as the "Three Rs": reading, 'riting and 'rithmatic. The monitors learnt the lessons and then delivered them with the children chanting the information, basic learning by rote. James Montgomery in Sheffield in 1807 provided this service for 4d (about 1p in decimal currency) per child per week.

Faith schools as they are referred to in the twenty-first century are not new, where there is a group of like-minded people the next step appears to have been a school. As mentioned previously the non-conformists and the Church of England had schools and so did the Jewish community. The London Jews' Free School started in 1732 is still going.

The town and church schools developed into the state system after the 1870 Elementary Education Act but parallel to these schools were private schools. Up until 1870 most schools were fee-paying but after this date these institutions remained though of differing standards, ranging from the long-established public schools to dame's schools. Anecdotally dame's schools were considered to be squalid, run by old women in dirty rooms but research shows that this was not always the case. Dame's schools as the name suggests were the domain of women but occasionally were taught by men. The basic syllabus was: reading, spelling, sewing and knitting. Most were a room in the dame's house and were an extension of the parent/child relationship and fitted easily into the lives of many working families. The standard varied widely; at worst they were a baby-minding facility, baby farms, and at best kindly, warm learning environments. The classes were small unlike the formal schools and the teaching methods more relaxed. A description of one was seen in an obituary in the *Sheffield Iris,* 5th September 1809 which noted the deceased, Mrs Hardy, aged 74

> "for the last 27 years kept a school in Copper St. where she instructed many thousands of little children in the mysteries of reading and spelling by a method of her own, peculiarly easy and expeditious. Among her pupils she went by the name of Giant Grumbo, her real name being unknown to most of her nearest neighbours till appearing on her coffin plate. Her school was numerously attended and from a humane consideration that when she was gone they might never get so good a mistress again. She preferred taking children of the poorest people whom she taught at the rate of two pence a week and would never raise her terms under any hardship of circumstances. Her integrity and independence of spirit were equal to her fidelity and skill in her humble profession. She lived alone and in almost entire seclusion, generally locking her door as soon as she dismissed her pupils."[16]

Children in dame's schools could come and go allowing them to help with the harvest or other family employment that needed them; toddlers accompanied their older siblings when there were no other baby-sitters.

So what about the dyslexics? How much would they have learnt in these different establishments with their differing methods? It is rare for teaching methods to be described, so to gain an overall picture it is necessary to put together scraps of information. It is known that young children used slates and slate markers rather than pens and paper as is recorded in literature as well as in diaries and reports of the time. Hornbooks were popular in the nineteenth century; these were bat shaped

---

16.   Malcolm Mercer, *Schooling the Poorer Child: Elementary Education in Sheffield 1560–1902*, 1996, Sheffield Academic Press, pp. 81–83.

objects with the alphabet on one side and simple texts printed on the other, also hard wearing and used as bats for bat and ball! The multisensory nature of scraping a slate pen across a slate board would have been beneficial to a dyslexic as would the constant repetition of the alphabet from the hornbook. However the habit of teaching reading without writing would have been less helpful. Some apprentice masters only paid for apprentices to learn to read as it was felt unnecessary for them to be able to write, and mathematics was a stage further still as mathematics lessons were paid for separately. By the 1800s formal schools taught reading followed by writing and the private schools taught both together. This made it difficult for any child to learn if they moved from one type of school to another.

A dyslexic in a large formal or state school would probably not have fared well though the standards of the time were not high. Nineteenhundred-and-four saw a final report written for the London School Board before it ceased, it covered the first years of state education (1870 to 1904) and the description of the standards of the elementary schools was damming. Prior to this date, in 1869, one of Her Majesty's Inspectors (HMI) complained that children were often in school for two years before they were tested making them at least seven. The test was required for a child to move to a higher grade and this of course meant that children left school at ten, seldom moving-up past the initial grade. The test by today's standards was almost non-existent: reading consisted mainly of narrating single syllable words, writing was copying one line of text, arithmetic was simple subtraction, addition and "the multiplication table". Girls also had to undertake plain needlework.

The inspector complained that many children spent their years in school hanging around doing nothing. In Sheffield in the late-nineteenth century the inspectors of the monitorial schools came to hate the sound of small voices piping lessons learnt by rote. Laurie Lee in *Cider with Rosie,* writing of the time just after the First World War, describes children leaving the village school he attended in Gloucestershire with only a few facts taught by chanting. Conversely, Margaret Penn reported in her autobiographical novel *Manchester Fourteen Miles* (written in the 1940s) of the fear engendered by the school inspectors both in the

31

teaching staff as well as the children if they did not reach the necessary grades in that year's tests.[17]

Joyce Morris, an educationalist, declared that the teachers in 1870 could only just read themselves; this was a generalisation but the tests of ability as seen were limited. She was correct in her opinion that teachers in the state system were also not necessarily trained to a high standard. The state system in England and Wales grew out the plethora of schools provided for the working-classes. These schools were fee paying but the cost was low and in some cases free but at such a cost the classes were huge and taught by monitors who were the oldest pupils trained to teach by teacher masters. The pupil teachers were like apprentices learning their trade from the headteacher or in larger schools a senior teacher. By 1904 we learn from the London School Board report of the training of pupil teachers that the Reverend John Rodgers set up the London Pupil Teacher System in 1846, recognising the problems seen by apprentices in London. Apprentices in general were better off outside London as they lived with their apprentice master, thereby living and working on the job, whereas the London apprentice had to travel from home to their place of work.

By 1870 there were two pupil teachers to each teacher. The pupil teachers were well-behaved and had a wide basic knowledge but had no depth of understanding and little intellectual capability to be imaginative. They worked for five hours a day and were often only 13-years-old or even younger. The headteachers who were meant to teach them had a full teaching load so often taught the pupil teachers early in the morning (as early as 7 am, a bad hour for all concerned). Rodgers tried to change this system by using 15-year-olds who it was hoped had a better overall level of education, and allowed teachers rather than headteachers as mentors. He recommended that the pupil teachers be taught in groups thereby allowing for more efficient instruction and they had time off for studying.

In 1874 Rodgers put forward his plans to the School Management Committee with the exception that his recommendation of a starting age of 15 was lowered to 14. The main features of the scheme were passed

---

17. "Payment by results" was still feared and spoken of in training colleges in the 1960s.

in February 1875. Candidates were to be over 14 and should have a six months probationary period. There was to be no evening class work and the pupil teachers were to work with a responsible teacher for the first three years of their apprenticeship. Pupil teachers were to be instructed in schools grouped together and payment for the courses was to be awarded by central government based on the examination passed by candidates. This examination, originally called Queen's/King's Examination and later renamed Preliminary Examination, took place after three years of training and education when the pupils were 18. If the pupil did well they were able to go on to a training college for a further two to three years. However, Rodger's plan, unsurprisingly, was watered down due to lack of funding. In 1846 16 centres were set up in London to train the pupil teachers and their fares paid by the London School Board, Similar centres were set up around the country.

In London the next progression in the training process was to have pupil teachers taught at selected schools by certificated teachers two evenings a week, allowing the pupil teachers to leave school early on these days. Students from non-board schools (the private sector) were also taught free or for a small fee, which was probably illegal but generally ignored because of the benefits to the community. Although the scheme appeared to be an improvement on the monitorial system and on the early training programme the workload placed on the young people was too heavy. Only the brightest pupils benefited, the pass rate went down, as did the numbers in training. The programme was altered to allow all candidates to have time off from school using the junior pupil teachers to cover for the senior group. The pupil teachers also had to attend on Saturday mornings.

Rodger's scheme cost more than was expected and a move was made to rescind the project. It was also felt that the pupil teachers were more interested in learning than teaching, and candidates were lost to other professions. The proposed changes were not carried but were put forward again in 1886. The alternatives suggested included schools staffed only by qualified teachers and assistants. This was approved as a satisfactory scheme but rejected on the grounds of cost and availability of assistants. An alternative was to revert to the original position of using headteachers; this was rejected as was the re-establishing of evening classes as it was considered to be too much pressure on 15 to 17-year-olds who were mainly girls. The final suggestion was to keep the present scheme, which was agreed with the proviso that there would be frequent reviews. The committee hoped in time to defray some of the costs from grants from the government, plus making the pupil teachers work for a reduced salary in their first year as assistants.

This snapshot of the growth of pupil teachers is just of London (1875–1904) but it mirrors ways of doing things throughout the country, which developed into certificates from teacher training colleges and teacher diplomas from universities. Hilda Morgan writes in 1916 of working with two dynamic teachers and being awarded a student teachership for one year before being old enough to enter teacher training college.[18]

Some teacher training colleges were established as early as the mid-1800. These were mainly instigated by the Church of England, non-conformist churches and Roman Catholics. Roehampton University is an interesting example as it absorbed under one umbrella: Whiteland's Church of England College,[19] Digby Stuart a Roman Catholic foundation, Southlands Methodist College, and the Froebel Institute which followed the teaching of Friedrich Froebel. All these colleges started in the mid-nineteenth century and continued to teach students to certificate level. The Second World War shook things up as the London colleges all left London because of the bombings and when they returned the world had changed. One of the changes was the vast numbers of students training to be teachers.

But of course this cannot be the only story; many children had excellent teachers be they their mother, tutor, class teacher or graduate teacher. Many children with mild forms of dyslexia would have coped because up until the mid-1800s it was possible to get by with a fairly limited ability in literacy. Most bright dyslexics could have foxed the London inspectors by learning the answers to questions beforehand, coping but not reading. It is, however, easy to forget how high the standards were in some schools, Tudor scholars could read in Greek and Latin and many

18.   Grace Horseman, *Growing Up Between 1900 and 1920,* 1996, Cottage Publishing.
19.   Whiteland's College was the first ladies teacher training college, originally located in Chelsea.

children by 1865 were well-versed in all elements of education so it was not surprising the Percy's teachers were worried about him. To modern eyes just looking at old books and seeing the small, dense print, with few illustrations or prompts to reading, our ancestors are to be admired. It is unlikely that many dyslexics reached high standards of reading, but relied on their wits to get them by.

By the late-nineteenth century, literacy was incredibly important and was a necessity in the workplace, and the industrial revolution had built a whole class of workers whose activities revolved around recording information. Charles Dickens graphically described places of commerce where rows of young men sat using beautiful copperplate writing. Women too were working in "offices" as it was acceptable socially for far more woman to work for a living. Outside of the workplace reading was as important as the ability nowadays to use a computer and the internet. All forms of reading material were readily available. Public libraries were introduced under the Public Libraries Act 1850 and, through sponsors like Tate, libraries were built. Novels were commonplace and more people had the time to read them. Newspapers were now more affordable but they were still outside of the average person's pocket. In 1855 they became affordable for the many, magazines became popular and "how to do it" manuals such as those made famous by the Beatons were read and enjoyed by all classes. Not only did the lady of the house read the latest publications and look up recipes in Mrs Beaton's *Book of Household Management* but so also did her downstairs maid. Song sheets were available at a cheap price and many made their own entertainment and had their particular party piece to be sung at family and friends' gatherings. Not forgetting of course the religious tracts, which were given away and were easy-reading. Not only was it fun to read it was also necessary to do so to survive in 1870s Britain, roads had names, buses had destination boards, trains had timetables and they all had to be read.

So if Percy found it difficult to read he was not normal and it would not have been so easy to disguise his disability. As people moved away from their immediate families their normal support systems were not readily to hand. The growth of the suburbs in the late-nineteenth century saw young families isolated. Help was not readily available from granny or uncle for the simplest of tasks such as baking, gardening and wood-work, and this must also have applied to help with reading and writing. Added to these worries would have been the fear and stigma attached to mental health problems. The language used about non-reading children right into the twentieth century sets twenty-first century teeth on edge: feeble-minded, retarded, simple, are three of the kinder terms. Emanating from laws passed as early as the fourteenth century the terms *lunatic* and *idiot* have huge legal effect; both would mean that an individual lost control of their own money and, in the case of the *idiot,* family monies were passed to the state/parish to support the individual. Parental concern for their child continued well into the twentieth century and as late as the 1970s parents had to hand over the decisions on where a child was taught if they accepted a statement of educational need.

By the late-nineteenth, early-twentieth centuries education was available to people across all social classes and although originally reading may have been the province of the aristocracy and clergy, even in Roman times, now some ordinary people had the ability to communicate through letter writing. Any "likely lad" or lass could learn to read and write given an element of luck; but as today the ability to obtain a good standard of literacy, whatever class, depended to some extent on where you lived. If a benefactor was interested in literacy be he nobleman or craftsman there would have been the opportunity to read. This pattern now called the "postcode lottery" has repeated itself through the centuries. In the main the very poor always missed out and to some extent this was literally a matter of lack of time as much as lack of money, but as seen above even those young people were helped by the nineteenth century through the setting up of foundling, industrial and ragged schools as well as the Sunday school movement.

One final question must be whether there was any help for children with learning problems? The answer is yes, disabled children were taught and the methods used can be seen in those now used to teach dyslexics.[20]

The deaf and blind were the earliest disabled groups to be trained. Training is the operative word as most deaf and blind children were taught a skill only so that they could earn a living, though some of these children through their own endeavours were educated to a high level. Examples of deaf and blind children being educated can be found in Europe pre the seventeenth century, but the growth of institutions for both groups only appear in Britain from the seventeenth century.

John Wallis is considered to have instigated teaching the deaf in England; he was a mathematician and forerunner of Newton at Cambridge. Interested in how language was put together, he wrote a book on English grammar in 1652 with an analysis of speech sounds, and he attempted to teach deaf people to talk by showing them how the different parts of the mouth make different sounds. (Making a child aware of how sounds are made has become an intrinsic part of teaching dyslexic children to read.) Wallis also constructed signs and finger-spelling as a forerunner of sign language.[21] The London Asylum for the Deaf and Dumb was established in the late-eighteenth century by the Reverend John Townsend with the help of Henry Cox Mason another clergyman and Henry Thornton a banker.[22] Townsend's interest in deaf children began when he was made aware of a deaf boy who lived in his parish. His mother had sent the boy

---

20. "The statutory foundation of special educational provision for handicapped children was laid in the last decade of the nineteenth century and remained broadly unchanged until the Education Act 1944. The Elementary Education (Blind and Deaf Children) Act 1893 obliged every school authority to provide education for blind and deaf children between the ages of 7 and 16 resident in the area in some school certified for the purpose by the Education Department. The Elementary Education (Defective and Epileptic Children) Act 1899 empowered local authorities to provide for the training of physically and mentally defective and epileptic children. These powers were made mandatory for mentally defective and epileptic children by further legislation in 1914 and for the physically handicapped by the Education Act 1918. Compulsory education for children suffering from these defects was extended to 16 under the Education Act 1921. Special educational provisions were re-enacted in sections 33 and 34 Education Act 1944 and modified in subsequent Acts of 1948 and 1953. New procedures were laid down in the Handicapped Pupils and School Health Service Regulations 1945 and later regulations". See http://www.nationalarchives.gov.uk/records/research-guides/special-education.htm
21. Gillard D, *Education in England: A Brief History,* http://www.educationengland.org.uk/history/
22. The Asylum for the Support and Education of the Deaf and Dumb Children of the Poor was established in 1792 by the Reverend John Townsend (1757–1826) of the Jamaica Row Congregational Church in Bermondsey, London.

to Thomas Braidwood's school in Edinburgh. Braidwood (1715–1806) established an academy in Edinburgh where he taught boys to lip-read.[23] Braidwood moved to London where he set up an asylum and taught with his nephew, Joseph Watson, who later also served as the superintendent. Townsend was secretive about his methods but Watson was more open-minded than his uncle and published their teaching methods in *Instructions for the Deaf Dumb* (1809). The school started with six boys but by 1804 had grown to such an extent that, with the patronage of the Duke of Gloucester, the asylum moved to Old Kent Road, London in 1807. The new institution was completed in 1810.[24]

For blind children the emphasis was also on training children to be self-sufficient and the most common skills taught were basket-making and piano tuning. However some attempt was made to teach the young blind to read. Teachers assembled raised letters that could be read by the blind through their fingers. Nicholas Sanderson contracted smallpox when he was a year old and this left him blind and he taught himself to read by feeling the tombstones in the local graveyard. Sanderson became a mathematician at Cambridge where he devised gadgets to aid the blind with calculus. The most famous person in the blind world was of course Louis Braille. He came from a modest French background and, unusually for early-nineteenth century France, his family could read and write. He was the fourth child of a saddle maker and in 1812 at the age of three Louis injured his eyes in an accident while playing with his father's saddle making tools. Through local patronage Braille was sent to school in Paris, the descriptions of which are reminiscent of Dickens' *Dotheboys Hall*. The pupils learnt to read using embossed books invented by Valentin Haüy. He developed a method of embossing thick wet paper using special letter presses. The resulting books were effective but heavy to work with and slow to read as well as to make. Braille, although young, began to play with the idea of making raised constructions using a code instead of letters. Braille's life reads like an adventure story taking place as it did during the French Revolution and the resulting wars. He met

---

23. Teaching the deaf in Britain depended on teaching them to lip-read and to speak, whereas in America, in particular, the deaf relied more heavily on signing which is the accepted way for deaf people to communicate now.
24. https://jaivirdi.wordpress.com/2010/06/14/the-london-asylum-for-the-deaf-and-dumb/

with Charles Barbier de la Serre probably at the Museum of Science and Industry in the Louvre where the blind students were demonstrating their reading.

Barbier was working on a method of sending and receiving messages at night; and so as not to alert the enemy this had to be undertaken in the dark. Braille immediately understood the possibility of combining his raised code with Barbier's invention, but it took him many years to refine the system. Louis Braille sounds like an amazing man, teaching blind children all his life, ill for most of that time because of the poor conditions of the school he attended and worked at. It took until the 1870s to produce an efficient typewriter that could produce what became Braille.

In teaching the blind their teachers and trainers relied heavily on the sense of touch but also on hearing. Audio-books for the blind are of course a pivotal method for blind students studying today and are also useful for dyslexic students. Physically disabled children who have no learning problems can be taught with a little ingenuity but for those with learning problems the story is different. These children were known as "idiots".This word may merely have meant any person outside of the norm but of course this came to mean unteachable—an echo of this idea reverberated down through the years.

Education opinions started to change in the eighteenth century and philosophers talked of pure education. Rousseau was particularly influential in this field and he put forward his philosophy of "child centred" education in his writings about a fictional character called Emile. Rousseau influenced educators like Pestalozzi and Froebel and they in their turn influenced Montessori. Montessori however also based a lot of her work on the philosophy and teaching of a man called Edouard Seguin who wrote a manual for teaching the disabled: *Idiocy: And its Treatment by the Physiological Method* (1907) The book is a point by point teaching manual for the disabled. Starting with the infant it continues through all stages of childhood to the young adult. Seguin takes the reader in minute, exacting detail through a multi-sensory teaching programme with step-by-step advice on how to train a child to move, to think, to appreciate sounds, colour, music and how to learn and thereby fulfil the individual potential of each child. It is a difficult read, mainly because of the detail but also the language of the time. *Idiocy: And its Treatment by the Physiological Method* must be the basis of "child centred education" and therefore influenced the conductive education movement of the sixties,[25] and just about every educational movement since.

Montessori in her book *The Montessori Method* acknowledges Seguin and said that though many quoted him she thought few actually read his work or carried through his programmes. This is understandable purely because of the time and effort that would be needed to work so intensely with a child. I was transfixed by the description of how to teach a child who could hardly move to climb a ladder. Picture Seguin moving the child up the ladder, with the child on one side of the ladder and the teacher on the other holding the child's hands and feet so he couldn't fall but so that he could also feel the weight of his body. Later in the manual Seguin describes how a mother should look into the face of her baby checking for signs of abnormality and if finding them acting immediately so as not to waste precious teaching time thereby being both loving and realistic.

Montessori did use Seguin's methods, originally with groups of children, who she was working with in an asylum. By working painstakingly through the manual she enabled the group to sit public exams. Using the lessons learnt from working with these special needs children she put together teaching methods that could be used with any child and this became the basis of the methods still used in Montessori Schools.

Possibly the last link in the chain leading to the multi-sensory teaching methods adopted by the Word Blind Centre was the teaching of the blind deaf. Probably the most famous blind and deaf person was an American Helen Keller whose story became a film and much has been written about her life. Annie Sullivan taught the rebellious young Helen how to speak and then read, Helen, with help from Annie, went on to achieve a high level of education. Annie taught Helen by tracing letters on her hand, the first word she learnt was 'doll'. She did this as Helen held the actual toy, painstakingly building up a vocabulary. In teaching these children the teacher needed immense patience, building a multi-sensory

---

25.   András Pető born in Hungary 1893, d.1967.

vocabulary of minute steps to aid the child's understanding and memory thereby enabling them to read and comprehend the world. In her later years, Helen worked with Grace Fernald and wrote books and articles on the subject of kinaesthetic learning. Grace Fernald was prominent in the dyslexia movement from the beginning and was researching dyslexia at the same time as Samuel Orton as will be seen later.

The deaf blind children also appear to be the link between the work being undertaken in America and in Scandinavia. Ragnhild Kaata of Norway (1873–1947) was the first reported case of a deaf blind child being educated and was well-known to teachers in America.

So back to the beginning, why were Percy's parents and teachers worried about him in 1896 when other parents possibly had not been before this date? Schools were available from as early as the first millennium, only to a few children but they were there and by the end of the 18th century schools were numerous and varied. Reading material was more scarce until the printing press, but pamphlets, books and letters were in common use from the 16th century. Class was a barrier to learning to read and write but a surprising number of children were educated from all classes though they were dependent until the Forster Act in 1870 on a well-wisher. Whether it was necessary to read until the nineteenth century is a moot point as although many could read many could not.

By the end of the nineteenth century Percy's teachers and his parents would have been aware of the stigma of not reading in a literate society and would have wanted him to go on to secondary education and university. From looking at documented dyslexic families' young dyslexic adults they did go to universities and enter professions prior to 1870 but perhaps the last straw for many was the introduction of timed examinations also in 1870 in most major universities. Until this point candidates could take their exams at their own pace but maybe the thought of this pressure spurred Percy's parents to take action.

From Percy to Peter

CHAPTER TWO

What Happened After Percy?

Just prior to the flowering of interest in word-blind children, scientists were looking at the brain and attempting to work out which bit of it did what. Two French surgeons, Jean-Baptiste Bouillaud (a phrenologist) and Paul Broca (an anthropologist) undertook post mortems on the brains of stroke victims who had lost the ability to write and speak and noted a softening in the frontal lobe. Broca continued to collect similar cases, one of his patients could only say "Tom", a name by which he was remembered. Macdonald Critchley wrote that in 1865 Broca realised that when the left side of the brain was affected the whole brain was not. Critchley also noted that, in France, Marc Dax had seen, as early as 1800, impairment in speech due to lesions in the left side of the brain. The scientists adopted the term "aphasia" for lack of speech and "agraphia" for the inability to write.

A professor of medicine at University College London, Dr W D Carpenter, coined the term dysphasia for the interruption of speech after an illness. Two German medical officers Gustav Fritsch and Eduard Hitzig carried out macabre experiments in 1870 on a battlefield in Sudan. With a portable galvanic battery and an electric probe they prodded the exposed brains of casualties to see what effect electrical stimulation had on the brain of injured soldiers. They followed up their observations by looking at gunshot wounds to the head and repeated their original experiments on the brains of dogs. One of their followers was Carl Wernicke and he is considered to be the first person to use the term "visual aphasia" or "word-blindness". In 1873, Wernicke had worked with a stroke victim, and although the man could speak and his hearing was unimpaired, he could barely understand speech, or the written word. These researchers saw the different functions of the brain as being set in a particular area. It took many decades for the researchers to see the brain as more plastic and mobile with many interconnections as now seen with the aid of imaging devices. Although John Hughlings Jackson, by 1891, was convinced of the "plastic brain", Jackson also worked with Sigmund Freud who started his career working on the physical brain before moving to psychoanalysis.

Dr F E Bastian a neurologist and biologist founded in 1887, with others, the Neurological Society of London and there he debated with Louis Pasteur, Charles Darwin and Aldous Huxley. Henry Bastian is said to have told a story of a butcher's boy who had never learnt to read and could only write his own name, but could remember his round and memorised 14 or more orders accurately each day without writing a list. Bastian is sometimes said to be the first person to report a word-blind child, through this story. But probably a school medical officer, Dr James Kerr, was the first. Earlier than Pringle Morgan's account in 1896, he wrote of "mentally exceptional" children with peculiar problems writing and reading but who could be taught in normal schools if their teachers took into account their "peculiarities".

As seen, Hinshelwood and Pringle Morgan had exchanges of articles and letters resulting in several other medical men writing articles and papers quoting similar case studies. However at this stage in the story it is worth looking a little longer at Dr James Hinshelwood; he was a Scottish eye doctor who had a particular interest in acquired word-blindness in adults. In his early articles on the subject he described the symptoms of brain damaged adults who, although previously literate, had lost their ability to read and or write and that had triggered Pringle Morgan's article. In *Congenital Word Blindness,* Hinshelwood looked back over 15 years of practising; in 1900 he had seen on two separate occasions boys with almost identical symptoms to each other and to Percy. They were bright with good memories, good at mathematics but unable to read. Their fathers had sought help from Hinshelwood because he was by 1900 known to have an interest in these unusual children who in the main were boys.

Seen through the literature, Hinshelwood is pivotal to search into word-blindness yet seems to come across as pompous, but one cannot fault his attitude to the word-blind children sent to him. He made it clear how wrong it was for word-blind children not only to be ignored but also not taught adequately. For Hinshelwood the condition was not as rare as his fellow researchers were saying and that at the best word-blind children would underachieve but at worst they could:

"…be harshly treated as imbeciles or incorrigibles, either neglected or punished for a defect for which they are in no way responsible where with dedication and persistence on the part of their teachers they could overcome the problems." [1]

Most of Hinshelwood's case studies looked at middle-class families; the wording was always "the boy was referred by his father". He alludes to the similarity of all his cases and those reported by other doctors. The subjects were mainly boys, all of about the same age, eleven to 14, so having been in school for some years they were all intelligent enough to have learnt other subjects, particularly mathematics, without being able to read, Hinshelwood argued that therefore they should have mastered reading. All the children had been tested for more obvious disabilities i.e. in eyesight and hearing and found to have no problems. By necessity Hinshelwood's cases were predominantly middle-class as he would have charged for his time, the National Health Service (NHS) not being in existence.

Although the majority of the articles written between 1895 and 1920 were by ophthalmologists some were written by school medical officers. One in particular, C J Thomas writes of "lower-class" children quoting eight cases in some detail. [2] The patterns of Thomas' case histories are the same as in other articles, otherwise bright children who just couldn't read. He also noted that the same problems also occurred amongst siblings, parents, uncles, aunts and grandparents. In 1905, Thomas went through the case histories of the London County Council (LCC) special schools

1.   James Hinshelwood, *Congenital Word-Blindness*, 1917, H K Lewis and Co Ltd, London, p. 43.
2.   C J Thomas, "Congenital Word-blindness and its Treatment", *Ophthalmoscope*, 1905, 3, p. 380.

and collected 100 cases of "congenital word-blindness" twenty-four of whom were girls the rest boys. As a medical officer he had followed some of the children over several years. Interestingly he states that due to the work of Hinshelwood, Nettleship, Stephenson and James Kerr, head-teachers from LCC schools were expected to refer to a medical officer any child who at the age of seven was unable to read

"…who appears very backward or defective; and in this way a great number of cases of word-blindness have been brought to light…there are now nearly 100 instances of the condition noted in the case books at the special schools for the mentally defective."[3]

It is amazing to think that these London children were being tested and treated for dyslexia at the beginning of the twentieth century.

Thomas thought that more word-blind children were present in the "lower-classes" than in the middle-class private schools, however it is more likely that children in private schools were noticed earlier due to the smaller class sizes and given help and the milder forms of the condition were overcome with good teaching. The state schools had large classes and there was less support from home.

Thomas is quite upbeat as to the future of the children he came across. He thought the bright ones from good homes would "pass muster" and quoted a surgeon friend of his who never read a book while training and learnt his trade via lectures and "grinds".[4] He is less hopeful of the less intelligent with poor backgrounds and thought they would be better concentrating on manual labour.

Many of the articles on word-blindness list the symptoms, and possible reasons for the condition but how to help the children is not discussed, however this is not the case with Hinshelwood, Dr James Kerr and C J Thomas. In Hinshelwood's *Congenital Word Blindness* the last chapter is devoted to methods he had used to help children. He was particularly incensed by Mrs Hume Pincent who at the conference of the National

---

3.   Transactions, Ophthalmological Society of the United Kingdom 1910, vol. 30 p. 223.
4.   "Grinds" is still used in Ireland to mean private tuition, and fictionally it is noted in Charles Dickens' *Hard Times*.

Special Schools Union in Birmingham in 1910 in a paper on "The Results of Special School Education" talks of Hinshelwood's case studies and comments like Thomas that children who were from elementary schools should be allowed to sink. Her reasoning was logical if cruel: as the classes were huge, 50 plus, it was unlikely that a child would be noticed as not reading and writing, especially as word-blind children were and are noted for being able to memorise their readers and copy accurately. By the time they were recognised as illiterate, years of learning had passed and Mrs Hume Pincett thought it was unlikely that they would ever catch up. Hinshelwood considered this to be defeatist and was not willing to give up on children that were referred to him. His recommendation was that word-blind children should be taught individually as in class they were too easily distracted, but as in the state system this level of teaching would be impossible he advocated using the child's parent.[5] He wrote that all of his parents including the poorest saw the benefit of their child being able to read and were willing to give their help. He could not accept the idea of a child not being able to experience the pleasure of reading.

Hinshelwood doesn't give detailed teaching plans but he recommended a phonic programme and for some children the "look and say" method.[6] He considered the frequency of the lessons to be most important, daily short teaching sessions and lots of persistence but also for the parent/teacher to recognise how tired the child would be after these intensive lessons. This method expounded in the early-1900s is exactly what is seen taught in America decades later and eventually brought back to England in the 1960s.

Thomas, like Hinshelwood, whom he quotes, thought word-blind children could be helped if taught individually and he too recommended a multi-sensory approach: concentrating on the shape and feeling of the letters of the alphabet to reinforce the sounds of each letter, building up a sound bank rather than relying on just the visual sense, which he considered to be the area of the brain that was damaged. He said letters

---

5.   James Hinshelwood, *Congenital Word-Blindness*, ibid, pp. 100–101.
6.   The "look and say" method was to present a child with a single word written on a piece of card in large letters. The child would *look* at the word, be told it and he or she would *say* the word after the teacher. This process would be repeated until the child remembered the association between the written word and the sound. Pictures were often used to support the words.

should be made large and bold and that wooden letters would be helpful.[7] Thomas introduces his readers to Miss Dale of the High School Wimbledon who believed in regular phonics.[8] Her methods were intensive and precise. Her revolutionary idea was that reading should excite children; unlike today the attitude at the beginning of the last century was that children should be "seen and not heard". Mrs Dale taught her girls (yes this time girls and not boys) that each letter was special, the little girls dressing letters in colours that suited each sound. When more complicated letter combinations arose the girls gave the group a name for example *tch* was called "the sneezing sister". When presented with a new letter the children recited the new letter aloud, they drew the letter in the air and drew/wrote it on a slate board before adding it to their letter/word bank which was written on the girl's blackboard kept in their desk.

For certain letters the girls were shown how the mouth made a different shape for each sound, "p" making a puffing breath against the back of the hand "b" being a little explosion. Drawing was also used to reinforce a particular letter. Miss Dale used only regular phonics in her early reading books and words that could be sounded out until the child had a good repertoire of words and was confident. Nellie Dale was famous in her day and produced series of readers, which are still in print.[9] She assessed each child after building a vocabulary of regular phonic words, as she knew they would then need to use their visual memory to progress. She built on the child's strongest sense, usually the kinaesthetic memory or sense to assist the weaker sense, which was often the visual pathway. She found that by using colour to differentiate letters this did not change the shape of the letters and so it was not difficult for the child to later transfer to normal text printed in black.

Working at the same time was Charlotte Mason who was recommended in an article by Herbert Fisher. He implied that Miss Mason used a "look and say" method of teaching, but it is probable that like Nellie Dale she combined phonics with "look and say" and based her

---

7.   Still used by the Dyslexia Institute in the 1980s and by Roman children millennia ago.
8.   Letters the sounds of which are "what you see is what you get", for example b a t = bat.
9.   Nellie Dale, *On the Teaching of English Reading: With Running Commentary on the Dale Readers — Steps to Reading; First Primer; Infant Reader.* First published in 1907 by George Philip and Son in London. Taken from Nabu Public Domain Reprint, 2011.

teaching on the same liberal principles and believed strongly in education for all. Charlotte Mason's books are also still in print and used by the home schooling movement. As with modern teaching methods for dyslexic children, Dale and Mason both advocated keeping the child's interest, keeping the lessons short and making the teaching child-centred. Neither teacher was specifically working with word-blind children but their approaches, which were methodical and well-structured, helped all children but particularly the word-blind. It is likely that both Mason and Dale's books and teaching methods were part of the American movement instigated by Orton, Gillingham and Stillman. Teachers through the ages will have tried every idea and trick to coax a child to read.[10] The difference between Dale and Mason and the ordinary but expert class teacher was that they passed on their teaching methods through training colleges and books. However being realistic Dale and Mason's methods required small classes and intensive teaching a luxury not available to state classrooms then or now.

Herbert Fisher another ophthalmologist writing in 1910 adds more cases to the growing lists of word-blind children. He wrote of one little girl who he had seen over several years for a sight problem who at the age of ten was not reading and he knew that this had nothing to do with her eyes. He noted that her reading improved when her mother taught her for 15 minutes a day but that she regressed when the lessons stopped. Fisher identified this girl as a good example of a moderate case of word-blindness and that she showed the necessity of individual teaching. Herbert Fisher also noted as many of the other writers had that word-blindness runs in families. He was sure that there were two categories of the word-blind: those who could not read or write; and those who had some difficulty in reading but had terrible spelling skills. He thought the children who couldn't read or write were brain damaged at birth while the other category had inherited the condition hence his interest the families of his patients.

The case of Master V H W a ten years old was referred to Herbert Fisher in the hope that his problem was one of eyesight but as with

---

10. A young relative of mine attended a small village school and the teacher there boasted that no child had left her school unable to read.

other cases his sight proved to be normal. The boy had been kept down in "the dame's class for reading"[11] and appeared, poor boy, to get everything wrong even down to singing the incorrect words in the choir.[12] Master V H W's father was an officer in the Engineers in India and his spelling was so bad that his wife had to check his letters and that his elder brother, also in the army, had the same problems; however their difficulties with literacy had not stopped them being successful in the army. Herbert Fisher was annoyed at only seeing Master V H W once, his interest being in his other siblings to add to his research.

Mr Treacher Collins in a discussion on word-blindness commented that he thought that children who were word-blind were often dismissed as stupid and that he was concerned that these children were

"often blamed, bullied, and laughed at, for a defect which was not his fault but his misfortune."[13]

It is not known how Percy felt about being dyslexic and prior to the 1960s there are few written accounts of dyslexia written by dyslexics. Ronald Hall coincidentally writes of his dyslexia in an article for the *British Journal of Ophthalmology*, "Word Blindness: Its Cause and Cure" (1945). The article as the title suggests describes what he considers to be the cause of dyslexia and a method to teach dyslexics to read but it is his harrowing account of being a schoolchild that grips the imagination. Ronald fought in the First World War and wrote that he would rather face the trenches than cope again with the classroom.

"Although in World War I, I spent over three years at the Front, I can truthfully say that I never during those years experienced a fraction of the stark terror that I did as a boy at the school during English lessons lest I should be called upon to read aloud and reveal to the whole class that I could not do so."

---

11. J Herbert Fisher, "Congenital Word-blindness (inability to learn to read)", *Transactions of the Ophthalmological Society of the United Kingdom 1910*, Vol. 30, pp. 126–222.
12. An interesting historical reference to schools pre the Forster Act of 1870.
13. Transactions, ibid.

Ronald developed tactics for side-tracking his teachers so that he would not have to read aloud, so scared was he of being ridiculed by his peers. He eventually learnt to read at the age of 15, and once he could do so rose to the top of his class

"from being nearly bottom at school to passing with ease top into a branch of the Civil Service where everyone who passed in below me had taken an honours degree at Oxford or Cambridge."

It took many years for Ronald to discover why he had found reading so difficult. He came upon a description of his disability in a psychology book and recognised his symptoms although even then the condition was not named, but through his links with ophthalmology he learnt to call it "word-blindness".[14]

Elizabeth Fry (1780–1845) did not write about her dyslexia but her writings speak for her. The well-known prison reformer left evidence of this in her unedited diaries; her spelling errors were numerous "intomit" for intimate, "peeple" for people.

Mainly the accounts of dyslexia are of famous people written by others. Thomas G West in *In the Mind's Eye* has put together a list of prominent people from Einstein to Leonardo de Vinci. I found one less well-known but equally influential character, Rupert Guinness heir to the famous brewing family who was severely dyslexic but survived Eton by being a good sportsman and of a "superb disposition".[15]

Up until as late as 1926 with the introduction of "talkies" in cinemas, films needed to be followed by reading subtitles, a problem one would think for the dyslexic. Joyce Storey in her autobiography comments on non-readers in the cinema:

"[S]ilent films were still with us and those who couldn't read the captions often had plenty of people around them to supply the story they missed."

---

14. Ronald Hall of HM Foreign Service, "Word Blindness: Its Cause and Cure", *British Journal of Ophthalmology*, 1945, pp. 467–472.
15. Rupert Edward Cecil Lee Guinness, Second Earl of Iveagh (1874–1967). Guinness awarded grants to the Dyslexia Institute Training Programme in the 1990s. I wonder if this was as a result of Rupert's dyslexia?

This can't have been easy for the non-reader, as we have seen with Ronald Hall, and Joyce records how her father suffered;

> "He had an inner strength and the ability to see, to understand and to care deeply. He could not express the things he saw or felt. Even to write was difficult and painful for him and my Mother did all the correspondence and handled all the money."[16]

Sybil Marshall in *Experiment in Education* writes of an eight-year-old boy who came late to her class. He was unable to read but also unable to do anything else. In what amounts to a case study, Sybil describes the boy's journey through learning and with an improvement in his family situation he became an intelligent member of her class and a good artist. However by the time he left school at 15 he had not learnt to read and from Joyce's description he appeared to be a classic dyslexic, but maybe because Sybil was a self-taught teacher she did not realise why he was not reading. Scarily neither did the educational psychologists who Sybil called in to see him.[17]

The dyslexia movement in the UK appears to stall in the second decade of the twentieth century. All the nineteenth century thinkers and scientist quoted by Hinshelwood and his colleagues were dead by the First World War: Adolf Kussmaul who wrote on aphasia died 1902, Wewrnicke died in 1905, Fredrick Batten in 1918 and Bastion 1915. Rudolf Berlin the German ophthalmologist who is now given the credit for inventing the term dyslexia in 1887 would probably also have been dead by 1914. Unfortunately so were James Hinshelwood and Edward Nettleship, who died in 1917 and 1913 respectively, they were in their sixties. Herbert Fisher and Sydney Stephenson died in 1933 and James Kerr in 1941. These thinkers who were so important in publicising dyslexia must have been greatly missed.

Nineteen-seventeen saw the end of the first stage of research into dyslexia. Critchley described it thus:

---

16.   Joyce Storey, *Our Joyce 1917–1939: Her Early Years*, 1992, Virago Press Ltd.
17.   Sybil Marshall, *An Experiment in Education*, 1963, Cambridge University Press.

"This period had been one of description and identification. Thereafter began a stage of analysis and discussion with a considerable amount of change in orientation. It also ushered in an era of uncertainty".[18]

Between the two world wars two women in Britain continued with the research into dyslexia. They were Lucy G Fildes and Margaret Macmeeken. Fildes article "A Psychological Inquiry into the Nature of the Condition Known as Congenital Word-blindness" is a research paper using 26 children.[19] In the article she set out to prove three theories: one that there was one area of the brain which controlled visual and auditory input, the destruction of which would destroy language; two that congenital word-blindness was one factor in a general lowering of "mental ability";[20] and lastly that there was a condition that lowered the "primary visual centres" which made reading and other visual based skills difficult. The subjects were taken from elementary schools (4) and schools for "mentally-defective children" (22). The children selected were tested with intelligence quotient (IQ) tests amongst which was the Stanford/Binet IQ test. Tests showed the children to be a varied group ranging from "morons" to those of superior intellect. The author noted that within the group the least able child's reading was more advanced than of the brightest child. All of the children were at least four years behind the norm and the best readers could not take dictation or spell.

Although Fildes' research covered recognition of letters, words and shapes which the children had been exposed to, it was also noted that reading is more complex than pure recognition and requires the reader to analyse what has been read and thereby interpret meaning.

In summing-up, Fildes noted that the children had a specific problem with reading and writing rather than a general learning problem but that this lead to general difficulties within all aspects of their studies. The research showed that there was not a single site in the brain responsible, so Fildes felt the condition could not be one of brain damage, and, although the condition of congenital word-blindness was specific,

18. Macdonald Critchley, *Development Dyslexia*, 1964, William Heinemann Medical Books Ltd.
19. Lucy G Fildes, *Brain*, 1921, vol. 44, "A Psychological Inquiry into the Nature of the Condition Known as Congenital Word-blindness", pp. 286–307.
20. The words in quotes are taken from Fildes' article ibid.

that it affected wider areas of both visual and or auditory understanding. Although the children often used visual imagery to assist memory Fildes felt that this did not mean they were strong in this area, some of the children had problems with visual input others with oral and some with both. Non-readers were found across the intelligence bands and the level of "defect" did not relate to the intelligence of the child but the lower the intelligence the more general were the children's difficulties.

Margaret Macmeeken like Hinshelwood was working in Scotland and in 1939 she looked at a group of 392 children in a large state primary school in Edinburgh in *Ocular Dominance in Relation to Developmental Aphasia*. The reasons behind the investigations were the concern felt by the W H Ross Foundation for the Study of Prevention of Blindness into the number of children presenting at eye-specialists who were unable to read adequately or in some cases at all, the same old story. These children had no problems with their sight so were sent back into the system with the presumption that they were of "low mental capacity". But Macmeeken considered that these children could be highly intelligent.

The study set out to look for reasons why some apparently intelligent children could not read. Macmeeken started by testing 900 children from state schools who were from roughly the same socio-economic group, their families were working people: in industry, shopkeepers, policemen, and railwaymen, most bringing in an adequate wage with only a few struggling to make ends meet. Many of the children also went to out-of-school organizations such as the guides, scouts and church groups. At home there was little cultural activity but all the families wanted to help their children yet had little idea as to how to go about the task.

The test threw up 392 children who fell into the category of low or non-readers, 194 boys and 198 girls. Further tests weeded out a group of children whose reading age (RA) was 15 per cent lower than their IQ. This group was made up of 15 boys and ten girls and their IQs were above 92 per cent, therefore of average or above intelligence, one of the criteria laid down by all researchers in this area. The children were tested individually and full notes were taken so a lot of data was collected. As with Fildes' study it was noted that a high IQ could mask a result, so the child might be reading at a reasonable rate but at a lower level than he/she should have been for their intelligence. As one would expect, being ophthalmologists, the researchers were particularly interested in the eye-conditions of the children and it was found that all of the subjects favoured their left eye.[21] When faced with word recognition some of the children could not even read small words but could recognise individual letters. The research team noted how the attempts at reading of ten of the subjects included lip and tongue movements,[22] facial grimaces and whole body movements. Blends were the big problem and there was some confusion over reversals both in the actual letters and in letters within words, e.g. *was* for *saw* and *si* for *is*. Macmeeken found that left-handedness ran in families as did reading disability. The age of the classes tested did not alter the incidents within a class nor the size of the class, which was a whacking 40–50 but some of the children tested were already on a "backward list".

In summary, Macmeeken and her team found that there were more word-blind boys than girls. That IQ had no bearing on the degree of disability. That external influences were not significant enough to be taken into consideration when looking at reading disability. The severity of reading disability ranged from mild to severe but was distinctive in character and could be categorised as "developmental aphasia" and that IQ alone could not determine the condition or emotional disorder as the latter was often present due to the inability to read well rather than other contributory factors. Macmeeken was concerned that intelligent children on the "backward register" could be there because they were word-blind but were being labelled as "retarded".

Macmeeken was aware of the research of Orton and Monroe and the teaching schemes of Fernald and Keller and indicates that her findings could be related to their work. She concluded that:

"The whole problem of these children, whom we have called *developmental aphasics,* is no minor one to be considered by educationists and administrators and as lightly shelved. The syndrome is a definite one, the incidence

---

21. A simple tube of paper or a hole in a sheet of paper was used to test the child's eye preference.
22. It was noted that when performing a task the child often displayed exaggerated tongue and lip movements. Miles talked of this in the interview and about his Phd students' work. Personally I have noticed that dyslexic students move all the time, such as swinging a foot or tapping.

is considerable. There can be no question that with regard to this group a serious responsibility must lie with our educators."[23]

It is said that at the death of Hinshelwood research into dyslexia moved to the USA. As just seen this is not absolutely true but work was taking place in the field in the USA and the chief thinker on the subject was Samuel Torrey Orton. Orton came across word-blindness as part of his clinical practice when working in 1925 in an experimental clinic set up by the Iowa State psychopathic staff in Greene County. Orton wrote:

"Among those children who were reported to the clinic by their teachers as 'dull, subnormal, or failing or retarded in school work' was a fairly high proportion whose chief difficulty was in learning to read. Two of these would fit Hinshelwood's criteria of true 'congenital word-blindness' and of these two cases (M P) also gave bizarre written productions."[24]

Orton had seen similar cases in adults with brain damage but he was convinced that the children were not damaged, rather they had a difference in the brain to do with the left and right hemispheres. He and his team went on to observed hundreds if not thousands of children, as did Marion Monroe working in Chicago. Their work was reported in articles and brought together in Orton's book *Reading, Writing and Speech Problems in Children* and Monroe's *Children Who Cannot Read*. Unlike the British researchers they went into a lot of detail about how dyslexia is manifested and described some of the more bizarre symptoms such as mirror writing. Unfortunately later the media took up this description and mirror writing became the most reported aspect of dyslexia. Amongst Orton's concerns was the problem that most dyslexic children have with reversals, for example they *b* and *d* and other combinations sometimes because they look alike as in *b/d* or because they sound alike as in *c/g*.

Orton died in 1948 and his wife carried on his work and started an institution in his name, which has been hugely influential in the

---

23.   M Macmeeken MA B.Ed, *Ocular Dominance in Relation to Developmental Aphasia*, 1939, University of London Press, pp. 49–50.
24.   Samuel T Orton, "Word-Blindness in School Children", *Archive of Neurology and Psychiatry*, November 1925, Vol. 4, No. 5.

treatment of dyslexia. Before leaving Orton it is interesting to look at his contribution to the naming of the syndrome. I have used the terms word-blind or dyslexic, the almost numberless names attributed to the condition will come later but Orton's "strephosymbolia" must take the prize for the most difficult both to pronounce and to spell. It literally means "twisted symbols", so is apt as a description of one of the main problems that Orton saw in children but what a mouthful.

From Orton and Monroe's work came a whole set of teaching programmes for the dyslexic. One of the most famous of these is that used by the Dyslexia Institute and was devised by Anna Gillingham and Bessie Stillman and is a multi-sensory programme. Kathleen Hickey brought this programme to England at about the same time as the Word Blind Centre started. It is difficult looking back after all these decades to see what was original and which learnt from other parallel teaching programmes. Charlotte Mason and Nellie Dale used a mainly phonic-based approach and in the chapter called "Questions" there is an explanation of the kinaesthetic methods undertaken by Grace Fernald and Helen Keller. In Denmark in the 1920s Edith Norrie, who was herself dyslexic, put together a teaching aid called the "Edith Norrie Letter Case".[25] This method bears resemblance to Nellie Dale's which may or may not have been a coincidence.[26]

The second pause in the research into dyslexia was of course the result of the two World Wars. The researchers were after all looking at a small group of children and adults and necessity moved the researchers into other fields of research as well as into the forces. For example, Macdonald Critchley changed direction from his work on aphasia when he was called upon to organize the neurological and psychiatric services for the Royal Navy.

After the enforced hiatus in dyslexia research it is puzzling as to why more research into dyslexia was not undertaken by educationalists. The

---

25. It is reported that Edith could not read her fiancé's letters so taught herself to read by splitting words into letters and sound groups (letter blends).

26. The Edith Norrie Letter Case is a teaching aid which is still being used: a box of individual letters and letter blends which are colour-coded and rely on the child seeing and feeling how sounds are made by the lips and mouth. The would-be reader chooses the letters from the box; the position in the box and colour of the letter blends correspond to the action of the mouth and lips. The box comes with a handy mirror for the child to see his or her mouth in action.

study into reading was active in the mid-twentieth century though this too had to wait until a larger proportion of the population could read adequately.

It is difficult for us to appreciate the lot of the average working-class child at the beginning of compulsory education. Our children are exposed to so much language through all forms of modern media but in 1870, for many children, especially those in rural communities, life was simple. To expect these children to be sophisticated readers was unreasonable. They needed reading to recognise animal stock lists, information pertaining to their trade, and simple religious tracts. By the mid-sixties training colleges, now grandly named "colleges of education", were busily teaching the mantra of "learning through play" and they had a point as how did a child get past the first post with reading and writing without language. Nearly 100 years before, the first aim of educationalists was attendance through compulsory education by 1904, in London attendance was at 80 per cent an improvement but still almost 20 per cent not going to school, a lot of children not learning.

The First World War and Second World War had exposed the appalling level of illiteracy among the working-class. The Second World War mixed up the classes and it was impossible for any one group to be unaware of another. Air raids forced people in towns to meet their neighbours in communal air raid shelters whereas previously it was possible to walk through poor streets without realising the level of poverty behind closed doors. Children were evacuated from big conurbations into the countryside and the authorities were forced to see the state of these children's health and education. The first wave of evacuees took place between 1–3 September 1939 and one and a quarter million women and children were voluntarily evacuated from major industrial areas, including the docks in London and Liverpool. The number was not solely children:

"735,000 unaccompanied school children and 166,300 mothers with 260,300 young children had been evacuated on September 1–3, as well as some 12,000 expectant mothers, 5,000 blind and cripples, and 71,000 others including helpers, physical and mental defectives in schools and hospital patients, making a total of roughly 1¼ million as against some 3½ million considered eligible."[27]

The evacuees came from overcrowded, deprived city areas and put a huge burden on the rural host families that took them in. The events caused such a scandal that society was forced to take notice. The report *Our Towns a Close Up* (A study made during 1939–1942) concentrated mainly on the physical state of the children and women but it notes that children from overcrowded areas were sleep deprived and the authors consider this to be the main cause of illiteracy amongst the group they call the "submerged tenth", a term taken from Charles Booth's *London Life and Labour* (1886–1903). To counterbalance the inadequacies of urban life many evacuees and their parents were appalled by basic sanitary facilities of rural dwellings, many village homes had no inside lavatories or running water.[28]

The programme of evacuation based on the estimated results of bombings taken from the First World War and the Spanish Civil War did not take into account the disruption to the children and families evacuated both to their housing and to education. Children were not forced to stay where they were sent and many drifted home or went to other safe places. The schools in the rural areas were over-subscribed, with local children learning for half a day and evacuee children the other half setting up an "us and them" situation. The children that returned home found their schools closed and used for other purposes and those that were functioning were grossly overcrowded.

Men "called up" were assessed not only for their physical state but also for their educational abilities and the shocking lack of literacy was brought home to the government. Out of necessity research into literacy involved testing and of course one of the spin-offs from the Second World War was the development of literacy testing. The dyslexia researchers saw IQ testing as well as testing reading levels as fundamental part of a battery of tests. The three main IQ tests that were used in the Second

---

27.   1942, Oxford University Press, pp. 1–2.
28.   Julie Summers, *When the Children Came Home, Stories of Wartime Evacuees*, 2011, Simon & Schuster.

World War were the Standford Binet Intelligence Scales, The Wechsler Intelligence Tests and the Ravens Progressive Matrix. On finding a high level of illiteracy amongst conscripted service men in 1939 it was decided to test the basic intelligence of all future conscripts. The Ravens Progressive Matrices (RPM)(developed by 1938) were adapted into a test which took 20 minute to administer and was routinely given to all entrants (conscripts) and this practice spread to many military services throughout the world (including in the Soviet Union) and continued at least until the present century.[29]

For the UK the World Wars were a turning point socially, and returning servicemen expected a different life. The level of illiteracy was the most obvious fact to be thrown up by both wars but by the Second World War this was not considered acceptable any longer and the Education Acts culminating in the 1944 Education Act stated clearly that all children, whatever their condition or place in society, were entitled to an education.

The resurgence of interest in education sparked greater awareness of the child as an individual and not just an underdeveloped adult. "Child centred" education meant that there was more awareness of how children learnt to read. Very few teachers were taught how to teach reading but bizarrely different methods of teaching reading became the current fashion. As today each method had advocates who would become fervent in their adherence to their particular theory and sometimes vitriolic towards those using a different teaching style. Joyce Morris in her article "Phoniscphobia"[30] writes of the almost rabid attacks on her for putting forward the use of "phonics" in the 1960s.

The main reading movements were: "phonics", "look and say" and "real books". Phonics is using the sound of letters and building the letter sounds into words, but this method only works for words that are spelt the way they sound (regular words). It also depended on the teacher and

---

29. John Carlyle Raven, who was probably dyslexic, invented the RPM as a non-verbal test and one that he found easier to administer than the Standford Binet test which he had been using to test children in East Anglia. This test could also be administered by parents or other non-professionals.
30. Joyce M Morris, "Phonicsphobia" originally appeared in the proceedings of the Literacy 2000 Conference, 18 September 1993: http://spellingsociety.org/uploaded_journals/j17-journal.pdf

the child pronouncing the letter sounds and letter bonds in the same accent and as clear sounds, without the urrr often heard at the end of a sound. "Look and say" is based on looking at a word and saying the word. This method works well if the word is illustrated with a picture, so a picture of a dog with the word dog. Obviously the child also had to learn the words that can't be seen i.e. *and, the, but* and this had to be learning by rote, not easy for a dyslexic.

Real books began as books written by a child about themselves using pictures they had drawn with the words describing the illustration. This method developed into using books that interested the child but were not written by the child. A spin off from real books was project centred teaching, this took an idea, event, theme and the children and teacher would work together on a project. In theory all elements of education, reading, writing and arithmetic would be covered during the reporting process with each child working at their own pace. Two exponents of the project method were Sybil Marshall and Sylvia Ashton Warner.

Sybil Marshall was an inspirational speaker and taught untrained for many years using an early form of child centred teaching. She captured her time in a Suffolk village school in *An Experiment in Education*. Her class of mixed ages and abilities lent itself to teaching each child as a unit allowing individuals to learn at their own rate. The experiment sounds from that brief description woolly but it wasn't and in the preface to a second edition of her book which came out in 1970 Marshall emphasised that each child might be a unit but they were still part of a class which at times had to be taught together. Also that the children did have to be taught by the teacher and not left to learn without any guidance.

In New Zealand Sylvia Ashton Warner taught Maori children in the early-1960s. She quickly realised that it was impossible to teach them adequately if she used western reading schemes. Her book *Teacher*[31] describes how she harnessed the oral culture of the children and let them produce their own books. The children would tell their stories (in the same way that English Primary School children share their "news"). These

---

31. 1963, Secker & Warburg.

encounters were often harrowing but Marshall felt the sharing to be a necessary part of integration, socialisation and an extended vocabulary.

Sybil Marshall, Sylvia Ashton Warner, Edouard Seguin, and Maria Montessori all did much to enliven and enrich children's experience in school. The methods were so seductive that it was easy for less experienced teachers to lose the thread and forget that the basics still had to be taught and understood. All teaching methods rely on the teacher, whatever the method, the system will be undermined if there is sloppy and inadequate provision of research materials and poor recording by the teacher. Some children just learn to read but others, dyslexics among them, need emphasis on one or more of the basic pathways to learning: auditory, visual and kinaesthetic to assist learning. No one method can stand alone but unfortunately fashion does not allow for this obvious point.

By 1960 much research had been undertaken into reading methods and most of it focused on "child centred" education. This clash with the work of the dyslexia movement was primarily because some teaching became chaotic and the two things a dyslexic child needs are order and structure. The environment of the classroom changed, gone were the rows of desks and in came informal arrangements of tables and chairs with children taught in groups. Depending on the politics of the school the groups were of mixed ability and some were of groups of children with a similar level of ability. Occasionally the groups were of mixed age and mixed ability, the argument being that each child should be seen as an individual. It was possible to teach these classes. Sybil Marshal would have born witness to this philosophy as would Sylvia Ashton Warner but for the average teacher it was a big ask. Classrooms were noisier places than they had been and children moved more freely than before. For most children this revolution was empowering but some children got lost especially in big classes and they went unnoticed.

The 1902 Education Act brought the administration of state schools in England and Wales under the care of local education authorities (LEAs) and enabled the establishment of secondary and technical schools and developed the existing elementary schools.[32] Church of England schools accepted state funding but in return lost some of their self-governance. The Education Act of 1918 put forward further reforms bringing the age of compulsory education from 12 to 14, encouraging further education.[33] Provision was made for those who could not pay so the inability to pay fees was not the barrier it had been. Fisher had envisaged nurseries for pre-school children and "continuation" classes for school leavers. However the between wars economic state of the country put a brake on educational reforms and it took the Second World War for the country to realise the need for an educated population, especially in technical education. It was seen that Britain was dragging behind Germany in educating its young people, an echo of times a century before which had galvanised the government into introducing universal education.

Although the country was at war thinking men and women worked to improve education culminating in Rab Butler's 1944 Act which changed the face of education in England and Wales. Many reports were written about major cities after the bombings but the lessons learnt from the evacuation project must have brought home the need to educate all parts of a child's mind and body. *Our Town Close-Up*[34] showed that a lack of literacy was not automatically the product of the poor unemployed families but also of overcrowded inadequate housing and parents who had not learnt good parenting skills. The children, it was reported, were often fed badly, given little or no fruit and vegetables and were not able or allowed to sleep properly.[35] Given time in the country with better food, room to play and a quiet place to sleep the children who stayed as evacuees (many went home as quickly as possible) improved and were able to learn and prosper. The report echoed Fisher's hopes for nursery education and parenting classes, money spent at the early stage in a child's life making much better economic sense than taking a child into care later.

---

32. The Board of Education established in 1899 previously had control, hence the term "board" school for elementary schools.
33. Sometimes called the Fisher Act after Herbert Fisher (1865–1940) who steered it through Parliament. Similarly the 1944 Act on this page is referred to as the Butler Act after Rab Butler (1902–1982).
34. Women's Group on Public Welfare, *Our Towns a Close-Up, A Study Made During 1939–1943*, 1943, Oxford University Press.
35. Scarily this report rings bells of current situations in some major cities.

Post-1945 many servicemen and women were able to enter further and higher education. They came from all walks of life and for the first time it was not acceptable when thinking of education for the social class of a child to come into the equation. Probably until the Second World War it was passable for a working-class child to be considered only fit for manual work but by this date so many working men and women received further education on being de-mobbed that they made it politically inconceivable to have these views. The lower, middle and upper-classes were still there but in many circles it was not "done" to recognise this fact.

Prior to the conference on the word-blind (1961) it is not clear as to why more teachers were not more aware of word-blind children. Probably they were just overworked and had little time to help all but the most severely disabled. The post-war classes were huge in the state sector. The increase in the post-war birth rate put the 1950s primary class sizes in the 50s and the 1960s primary classes were still over 40. Gone was the mixture of schools seen prior to 1870 in England and Wales (Scotland has always had a different education system to the rest of the UK). By 1944, not so many years later, a massive change had taken place. Local education authorities, set up in 1902, administered the rate levied to pay for the state education system. Private schools did not have the same level of inspection or necessarily the same standard of teaching and state schools regulated the size of classes, though most private schools had smaller class sizes than state schools. All state schools were inspected and teachers were trained and certificated. The government, influenced by the findings of those working with deprived children during the Second World War, organized school meals (free to some) and free milk.[36] The education and health ministries combined to regularly inspect children for general health. Most of the problems with illiteracy reported by those other than parents were from doctors seeing children referred to health clinics.

By twenty-first century standards the schools in the 1940 and 1950s would seem to be draconian but they were amazing when one considers

---

36. Each child received a third of a pint of milk in a small glass bottle with a straw. Baroness Thatcher removed this facility from seven to eleven-year-olds when she was Minister for Education (1970–1974) and a rhyme was sung, 'Maggie Thatcher, milk snatcher'.

what had gone before. In *Schooling the Poorer Child*[37] the author describes Sheffield schools in the nineteenth century where there was no direct sunlight in the classrooms and this must have been common in many industrial areas. Playing outside in town schools was unheard of before Matthew Arnold's (1822–1888) theories were enacted and playgrounds were made part of schools. The Victorians built big elementary schools with the infants on the ground floor and the girls and boys post-seven years educated separately on the upper floors, usually with segregated playgrounds.

When I went to school in the 1950s and when she started teaching in the 1960s most of the town schools were still in Victorian buildings, though by then classes and playtime was co-educational. The classrooms had high ceilings, with windows on to a central assembly hall as well as to the outside, and the headteacher would walk around the main hall looking into each classroom.

Hilda Morgan describes the school she went to in 1916.

"I went to St Michael's Church of England School. Miss Ashley, the Headmistress, we called 'Governess'. She sat at a desk on a dais in the centre of one side of the assembly hall, where she could oversee each classroom."[38]

The lavatories were outside and there were big playgrounds wrapped around the school. Of course many large city schools are still in these buildings but hopefully the internal layout has altered somewhat. In the 1950s the children sat in rows at wooden desks usually two children to each desk, sometimes with separate seats but often with a bench seat. Each child had a writing slop over a desk to hold books, exercise books, pencils, crayons and pens; and the desk tops still had inkwells. There were two or three blocks of desks with walkways for the teacher to move up and down. School could be frightening even in the 1950s with the teacher administering the slipper or the cane and pieces of chalk and

37. Malcolm Mercer, *Schooling the Poorer Child, Elementary Education in Sheffield 1560–1902*, 1996, Sheffield Academic Press.
38. Grace Horseman, *Growing Up Between 1900 and 1920*, 1996, Cottage Publishing. Coincidentally the school described is the one I started my teaching career at in Southfields, London in 1968.

board rubbers flew through the air hitting a child who was not concentrating, but with 50 plus children to a class life must have been grim for the teacher as well as for the child. Not surprisingly the dyslexic child disappeared in such big classes. The best that could be expected was that the "backward" child was sat in front of the teacher rather than at the back of the classroom.

One of the aims of the 1902 to 1944 Education Acts was to bring down class sizes but the authorities had not envisaged the explosion of births after the Second World War.[39] By the 1944 Education Act the overall welfare of the child was being catered for in much the same way as it is today. The process may not always have worked but the framework was there.

Were teachers interested in finding Percy? Mildly word-blind children muddled through. Although children in this category would not have reached their natural potential they learnt to read eventually and were euphemistically called "late developers". In many cases teachers did then as they do now and tried all teaching methods at their disposal to help "a Percy" to learn and there were many Miss Dales and Miss Masons who helped children with mild dyslexia without realising the cause of the child's reticence to read. However, reading between the lines there were references to children who had learning problems which could have been dyslexia. In the 1904 report to the London School Board it was stated that there was special provision for deaf and blind children and in 1891 the sub-committee responsible for the above had also taken on "special instruction for mentally and physically defective children". It was named the "Special Schools Sub-committee" and the 1903 Education (London) Act which extended the 1902 Act gave powers for children in that category to be educated. This provision will have been the result of inspectors in 1888 reporting that there were other groups of children who should be given special consideration and it was agreed that the "feeble-minded" be added to the deaf and blind.

"These are defined as children who, not being imbecile and not merely dull or backward, are by reason of mental defect incapable of receiving proper

---

39. Known then as "the bulge", known now as "baby boomers".

benefit from the instruction in the ordinary Public Elementary schools, but not incapable of receiving benefit from instruction in special classes or schools."[40]

The report defined children who were either physically or mentally unable to benefit from a standard education and who were to be educated separately. In 1892 two schools were set up in London to teach these children. It was expected that other large centres of population would also have such schools. The report on the results was glowing as many of these children re-entered mainstream schools and functioned adequately although they were often placed with younger children. The special school curriculum was less proscribed than for the standard school and taught handiwork and skills necessary for manual occupations. The number of children that were deemed to be "educateable" was estimated at eleven per 1,000 which is approximately the figure given for children with severe word-blindness.

If parents in post-war England were concerned for their non-reading children why were more educationalists not worried? From the end of the Second World War to the 1961 conference on word-blindness ordinary teachers had a lot on their hands. They were much better educated than their forbears but in the main they were not taught how to teach reading. It was felt that if a child was provided with the right stimulus and the means he or she would learn to read naturally. The teacher's job was to hear him or her practice this skill and provide the next book in the reading scheme to build on his or her learned vocabulary.

For most children this method worked, children do learn to read with no apparent effort but some children don't. In many cases this is because the child has not been exposed to language, so does not have the necessary tools — words — to read, for some their home background is chaotic and as such emotionally they cannot learn.[41] These were the children that the teachers of the 1940s, 50s and 60s were worried about. There will have been dyslexic children among these deprived children just as was seen

---

40. *Final Report of the School Board for London, 1870–1904*, 1904, P S King & Son.
41. In my first year of teaching in 1968 one child, a little seven-year-old girl would come for me to hear her read. She stank of urine because she would wet herself and her mother would dry her knickers rather than wash them. It was difficult to give the child the attention she deserved.

by Hinshelwood and his colleagues earlier in the century but attempting to rectify social wrongs and inadequacies were the post-Second World War teacher's priority. Parents however saw things differently and they were concerned for their individual child and set about singly and later in groups to find the reason for their "Percy's" problems.

CHAPTER THREE

The Pioneers

All innovation requires a team of dedicated people and the Word Blind Centre had such a group. Before discussing how the centre got off the ground it is instructive to look at the people who were involved. I was lucky to meet some of the pioneers and part of this chapter is taken from transcripts of my interviews. Many more people were involved than can be reported here but the following mini-biographies give a flavour of those who worked so diligently to help dyslexic children and later dyslexic adults.

When contemplating working on this project it was the people that grabbed my attention. Over time they had drifted into helping dyslexic children. Few made a conscious decision to take part and they came at the idea from different standpoints. One or two were dyslexic, others had dyslexic relatives but they had all seen the results of dyslexia even before they had given the condition a name. In trying to make a difference they had to swim against the tide because instead of helping all slow readers they wanted to help a small percentage who they felt had been misunderstood and who with help could go far. The problem was that by trying to help dyslexic children they appeared to be elitist. They seemed to be only dealing with middle-class children. In the 1960s, dyslexic children from the working-class had slipped a long way behind and for some it was too late to help. Tim Miles proved decades later that dyslexic children were found in all walks of life.[1]

---

1.   The BCS70 is a continuing, multi-disciplinary longitudinal study of 17,000 babies born between 5th and 11th April 1970 (estimated to be between 96–98 per cent of all births). Miles is not now involved, but he is still working on the data. This data has been archived but can be found at: https://discover.ukdataservice.ac.uk/series/?sn=200001 7/4/2016

The pioneers that I met or for whom I have found records had all previously been working with dyslexics even if not known as such as these children had many descriptions through the years, the kindest in the 1960s being "late developer". Whether through their writings or in face-to-face encounters, meeting the pioneers I was reminded what trailblazers they were although by the time I interviewed them they were quite elderly. They were part of the "swinging sixties", the world was changing, especially the world of education and they were determined that dyslexic children were not going to be left out. They may not have achieved all of their dreams but they had a good try. The minutes of the Word Blind Committee contain a wealth of information especially if one reads between the lines. The following mini biographies are just a taste of the mixture of people that worked at and influenced the Word Blind Centre.[2]

Grace Rattenbury

As in all organizations it was the administrators who saw to the smooth running of the centre. Grace Rattenbury GM, MA was the general secretary to the Invalid Children's Aid Association (ICAA), so was responsible for far more than just the Word Blind Centre; she was in post from the outset of the centre, her name appearing on numerous agendas, letters and memoranda until 1966 when she retired.

Rattenbury was a product of St Paul's School and New College Cambridge. She started work as a social worker in Liverpool and had begun working with the ICAA in 1927 where she helped start a branch of the charity in Bermondsey, and later another in Dagenham. It was in the East End that Rattenbury's action won her the George Medal as reported in the *London Gazette* of 7th February 1941. She was by this time also working as a volunteer for the Women's Voluntary Service (WVS).[3] Using a WVS van she shuttled women and children out of the Docklands area

---

2.   The view of them reproduced here is my own personal view.
3.   Later the WRVS. After the Second World War the WVS still operated because food rationing remained in place. Such was the work that it did, that the new Labour government funded the WVS from central government coffers. In 1956, Queen Elizabeth II agreed to become patron and ten years later, in 1966, she awarded WVS the honour of adding "Royal" to its title.

of London which had been severely bombed and where raging fires were blocking the way to the front line rescue centre. The only way out of the area was across a narrow bridge and the road was full of potholes and debris. Rattenbury risked her life and although she repeatedly had to take cover from bombs she stayed calm helping others not to panic and kept going until every woman and child was safe.

Rattenbury continued her war effort by working for the ATS (Auxiliary Territorial Service) where she served as sociological officer coping with social and emotional problems created by a massive organization brought about by the problems of war. She returned to the ICAA in 1948 to become general secretary just in time for the National Health Service. The ICAA had provided care for sick and disabled children and although the NHS would take over some of the functions undertaken by the charity there was still a necessary role for the ICAA and Rattenbury oversaw the transition. It is noted in her obituary that she helped the ICAA to continue, as a voluntary organization, to fulfil a need alongside the NHS.

> "She brought the Association through one of its most difficult and challenging periods, and the greatest tribute to her is that at the end of her period of office, it still retained its spirit of voluntary service, its high standard of integrity and though small has a reputation for solidly founded and efficient work of the type supplied by no other voluntary organisation."[4]

When Rattenbury died, in 1989, ICan (the current name for the ICAA) commented that she was a pioneer in women's employment but as the press release also said she helped to expand the ICAA's interests and assist in the "little known field of psychological illness in children" which can be taken to mean dyslexia.

Macdonald Critchley

Macdonald Critchley a neurologist who appears throughout this story sat on the committee that ran the Word Blind Centre and he also assessed

---

4.   Taken from the unpublished ICAA papers housed by the London Metropolitan Archive.

many of the children who were taught there. Critchley was an all-rounder; he was interested in the arts as well as his areas of medicine and was still writing until hours before he died at the age of 97. Although from a fairly ordinary background, his father was gas-collector, he was prodigiously clever and matriculated at age 15 from Christian Brothers' College, Bristol. He was too young to go to university so he started to study German. Britain and Germany were at war in 1917 so he changed this to Greek; he already spoke French and Latin. Bristol University accepted him when he was 16, but at 17 he joined the army as a private. His obituary tantalisingly mentions that during this period he was imprisoned due to a "technical infringement" and although he found this upsetting he later stated it was an experience he would not have missed. On being released he joined the flying corps as a cadet where he studied Russian. Back at Bristol University he achieved a first-class honours degree as well as acting in several of the theatres in Bristol.

Critchley specialised in neurology and within this specialisation he became interested in why some children found it difficult to learn to read and write. His first book on the subject was published in 1928, *Mirror Writing* and this became the basis for *The Dyslexic Child* (1970), for which he received the Sam T Orton prize in 1974.

Critchley's connections were important to the Word Blind Centre; he worked at Great Ormond Street Hospital for Children and the National Hospital in Queen's Square where the Word Blind Centre Committee were often to meet. Because of his breadth of knowledge and the universal recognition of his ability, doors opened for him. He was also well-liked, described as reserved, but he always took an interest in the person he was speaking to. His colleagues described him as a real gentleman, approachable and caring. Of all the writers on the subject Critchley most clearly describes what he called the "soft symptoms" of dyslexia. These are the irritating foibles that dyslexic people have to learn to live with. The chapter in *Developmental Dyslexia*, "Minor Neurological Signs", lists numerous difficulties experienced by dyslexics, from an inability to learn Morse Code and muddling "yesterday, today and tomorrow" to learning to tell the time, all of which require sequencing skills. With each illustration

Critchley religiously quotes the learned source for his example, teaching his readers in a determined, systematic manner.

Being a pioneer of dyslexia in the 1960s was not an easy ride and during the 1961 conference (see next chapter) he was heckled by educational psychologists who felt that neurologists had no right to be interfering in education. Critchley saw the waste that resulted from a dyslexic child not being successfully taught and was one of the first to comment on the number of young men in prison who were undoubtedly dyslexic.

Tim Miles saw Critchley as being from the upper middle-class, perhaps not being aware of his ordinary background, as when Miles knew Critchley he was horse-riding man and opinionated, but Miles had a lot of time for him. Miles concluded that Critchley saw dyslexia as a medical condition which to an extent freed him from the restrictions of the psychologists, being able to see across the spectrum.

His entry in the *National Dictionary of Biography* sums him up:

"Critchley's manner was that of the distinguished physician of the mid-twentieth century—quiet, elegant, unhurried, and always civil. An apparent aloofness of manner reflected a natural reticence which concealed from most a concern for others prompted by shrewd insight into their personalities. He avoided any unnecessary movement and counselled against exercise. In later years in his office in Queen Court, he would sit surrounded by cushions in an armchair at his desk, in the side-shelves of which were memorabilia of Oscar Wilde, pieces from his collection of paste jars, and curious objects collected in the Far East."[5]

Helen Arkell

Helen Arkell was the first teacher at the Word Blind Centre. She was one of the few teachers in England who had any experience of teaching dyslexics and she was an obvious choice when the committee were looking for teachers. An amazing lady, I was privileged to meet her in 2005 when she seemed to be totally unaware of the effect she'd had on

---

5.   W I McDonald, *Oxford Dictionary of National Biography:* http://www.oxforddnb.com/view/
     article/69194 28/04/13

so many lives. Arkell is dyslexic and understands the underlying problems of the syndrome.

Arkell first realised that she was dyslexic after the Second World War when she was reunited with her Danish family and learnt that her nephew had been diagnosed with dyslexia. Her nephew's difficulties and differences matched many of her own quirks and this was an explanation for her problems at school. On visiting her family in Copenhagen Arkell decided to seek help from the same person who had assessed her nephew, Edith Norrie. On her website Arkell talks of her first meeting with Norrie who was a daunting woman and how Arkell was amazed at how Edith understood her problems, and had seen them all before. As a result of this meeting and after some time adjusting to the information Arkell spent two months in Denmark staying with her sister and learning Edith Norrie's teaching methods and using the Edith Norrie Letter Case.

Arkell attended the first conference in 1961 though when I spoke to her she had forgotten this, but there she is in the conference report. By the time the Word Blind Centre started in Palace Gate, Arkell had been teaching dyslexic children (then termed word-blind) for some time. She only ever taught part-time at the centre as she still had clients in Frensham where she was and still is living. Arkell was shocked at being asked to teach for the centre. She deprecatingly told me that she had never passed an exam in her life, but she was the one who started the teaching and whose kindness will be seen in further chapters of this book.

Alfred White Franklin

Alfred White Franklin was probably the most important person in this saga. He was born in 1905, the child of a medical family. He was educated at Epsom College and Cambridge University gaining his medical qualifications from St Bartholomew's Hospital. After a year at John Hopkins University in the USA he returned to Bart's where he worked in paediatrics, particularly in the area of child abuse, this work continuing to be a priority for him until his death. In his papers he repeatedly mentions the children he saw with numerous physical problems but who also couldn't read. This worried him as it had Macdonald Critchley.

White Franklin too had interests outside of medicine. He was a co-founder of the Ostler Club and a member of the Athenaeum but he was also influential in the medical world heading up societies and publications. He kept up his connections with his American contacts both socially and professionally. These liaisons stood him in good stead when he began to bring the plight of word-blind children to the notice of the general public.

The buildings at Corams Fields, some of which would eventually house the Word Blind Centre, were also used in other areas of child care and White Franklin was involved with these, giving him inside information when the centre was looking for a home. In the late-1950s he sat on numerous committees all concerned with children, for example the National Bureau for Co-operation in Child Care. Members of these committees appear in the Word Blind Centre story: Kellmer Pringle; Baron (Henry) Cohen of Birkenhead. In 1951 he was appointed senior consultant paediatrician to Queen Charlotte and Chelsea Hospital.

Money raising also came within White Franklin's area of expertise and through the ICAA he became friends with Princess Margaret who helped to raise a lot of money for both the ICAA and the Word Blind Centre in particular. There are photographs in the White Franklin archive showing him and his wife at Princess Margaret's wedding as well as numerous other social occasions. Princess Margaret took a great interest in the Word Blind Centre and officially opened it on 12th October 1965.

White Franklin was no stranger to controversy and had an early interest in children with severe speech and communication problems; there are letters as early as 1960 showing his concern. The ICAA was responsible for opening schools to assist these children, John Horniman's in Worthing was one, but better known perhaps was Moor House School. It appears there was some in-fighting as to the best way of treating/teaching these children; similar to word-blindness, diagnosis was a mixture of physical and psychological problems. White Franklin's daughter Judy became a speech therapist.

Like Critchley, all spoke of White Franklin with awe but also affection. Known to his closest friends as "The Bishop" he was a short, portly man who dressed as an old fashioned medical consultant might. Wednesday was his day at the Word Blind Centre and he would be found there taking a picnic lunch with his colleagues. He continued to support the centre throughout its short life and was involved in the final conference and teaching sessions. His obituary in *The Times* summed him up:

> "Dr White Franklin's superficial conventionality was not the exoskeleton [outside shell] of a man unsure of his own convictions, nor was his genuine humility: he had a sly sense of humour expressed in a characteristic giggle, was a shrewd judge of men and affairs and right into old age was receptive and productive of new ideas."

Gill Cotterell

I was lucky enough to meet Gill Cotterell in 2004 and although at first she seemed a little scary her dedication shone through and I was taken up by her stories of the pupils she taught and how she had devoted her life to helping children and adults fulfil their potential. Like Helen Arkell, Cotterell did not appear to be aware of how influential and important she was to the dyslexia movement. Arkell had said that Cotterell came to the Word Blind Centre as a bit of a sceptic but like all converts once convinced was ardent for the cause.

Cotterell trained at the Froebel Institute, Roehampton and went on to teach mainly in private schools. In 1953 she worked in an international school in Switzerland and on returning to England had taught at a boy's prep school in Malvern and later, in 1956, at a state school in St Albans, then back to prep schools. It was while teaching in prep schools that she came upon a seven-year-old boy who was very bright but labelled lazy. This worried her and she wanted to learn more so undertook a diploma in the psychology of childhood at Aston, Birmingham and was taught by Margaret Newton. Cotterell talked to Newton about the seven-year-old who said he was almost definitely dyslexic. She later wrote her dissertation in the aftermath of researching a group poor readers (not dyslexics) as described on page 155. The youths were aged 16 to 27 years and referred to as "severe reading disabled".

The Word Blind Centre had just opened and Cotterell was offered a temporary post, a situation which suited her as, if she felt she wasn't happy, she was not obliged to continue. She was committed to a holiday in the USA and on board the boat by chance met Betty Warbetton who offered her temporary accommodation in Fitzroy Street. Cotterell happily found herself in central London and in the exciting new enterprise of the Word Blind Centre. The director at the time was Alex Bannatyne and she found him inspirational. Many years later she still spoke of him and his work with enthusiasm. Tim Miles said Bannantyne also started as sceptics, so two converts together.

Cotterell felt that the way to teach non-readers was to put writing and reading together. She got the child to choose a subject, just a word, that interested them and, as the student usually remembered the word they were interested in, success started in the first lesson. Helping them to see how to start to write a word as part of reading was much the same technique as Charlotte Mason used with her little girls. Part of Cotterell's equipment was the Edith Norrie Letter System and she also encouraged her pupils to draw.

Cotterell saw six children individually per day, each child had a 45 minute session and there were 15 minute breaks in-between to write up the activities of the session. Even decades later in interview it was obvious that she loved the children and had a good rapport with them. Many of the children had been ignored up until this time. A boy assessed by Bannantyne was the child of a farmer and was not at all receptive to studying; he could read but not spell. During an early session Cotterell and the boy met Roger Bannister, the first man to run the four minute mile. Bannister had been a young doctor when he was running and later became a neurologist and so had an interest in the Word Blind Centre. Gill seized the opportunity to gain the boy's attention and asked him if he knew who Roger was, and he said no, so Gill set him the task of finding out. On returning he had discovered a huge amount and put together a magazine about the runner. The boy later went on to university and married a speller![6] Cotterell left the Word Blind Centre in

---

6. A term commonly used in the dyslexic world to signify someone who, unlike dyslexics, can spell. A helper basically.

1967 but continued to work and study in the area of dyslexia (but more of that later).

Tim and Elaine Miles

I interviewed Tim Miles twice. He was one of the main influences for this work. I had heard him lecture a few times before I met him properly and even in a lecture room you felt he was talking just to you. He understood dyslexics, not a mean feat as every dyslexic is different to every other dyslexic. They may have some symptoms in common, however one of the most difficult aspects of being dyslexic and diagnosing dyslexia is the mix, but Tim understood this. I contacted him and asked if I might interview him and he invited me to Bangor where, in retirement, he and his wife Elaine had been given an office in a corner of the psychology department at the University of North Wales. I eventually found him, surrounded by filing cabinets and a computer screen with huge fonts, as by his eighties Tim's sight was reduced to tunnel vision. But this did not deter him and he and Elaine were still writing books and articles and helping people like me.

Miles' academic career coincided with the Second World War and he was called-up while at Oxford where he went up in 1941 as an exhibitioner to Magdalen College. His first degree was in Philosophy and Ancient History ("Greats"). Miles was deprecating about his war, he had been part of the Officer Training Corp at Oxford and because of this had gone straight into the army as an officer cadet and "never had to peal potatoes", rising to the rank of lieutenant where he stayed throughout his army career. During conversations with other young men, one of whom was a Communist, Miles came to the conclusion that he should be a conscientious objector. Unlike in the First World War this did not involve him being thrown into jail. Conversations and appeals went back and forth and in the end he was sent back to Oxford to see out the remains of the war.

In October 1945, Miles his head of college, called Jack Tizard, was sympathetic and supported him. His colleagues in the army were by now being discharged and if he refused to do non-combatant duties he too would have been dismissed; however the board said he had defeated them because of his stance. By November 1945, the war was over and someone must have "pulled strings" as he was told to go back to Oxford, where, of course, he had been since October gaining a few "undeserved months".[7]

Miles met Elaine at Oxford when they were both reading Philosophy and Ancient History. They met at a Gaudy Celebration, walked along the Backs, "one thing led to another" and they married in 1951. Elaine and Tim's partnership was important not only as a personal one but in their working lives together. Elaine trained as a teacher and this became a central part of their work and research.

After finishing his first degree Miles decided to undertake a second one in the new Oxford Department of Experimental Psychology. Oliver Zangwill was probably the first person he met; at the time Zangwill was a young lecturer in the department and he was to become an important force in Miles' life. Miles was offered a job at Bangor before his finals, and when he got there he and Zangwill stayed in touch.

Soon after arriving, Miles was given a day a week in the local child guidance clinic, he worked with a psychiatrist, a psychologist and a psychiatric social worker. On the very first day he was to meet the child who later he named "Brenda", one of the two children with learning difficulties who he wrote about in *Two Cases of Developmental Aphasia*. Miles discussed Brenda with Oliver Zangwill, who was encouraging as "the case was genuine and important" and he recommended reading some of the early literature on the subject. It was some years before Miles had a paper published in the *Journal of Child Psychology and Psychiatry* in 1961, but the results of this were to change his life and it is where our story begins. As a result of *Two Cases of Developmental Aphasia*, Alfred White Franklin invited Miles to take part in the 1961 conference on word-blindness.

Miles took an active part in the life of the Word Blind Centre. He was one of the psychologists but more importantly was on the committee that oversaw the work of the centre and he contributed to the bulletin which was the academic mouthpiece its work. He was a stickler for academic rigour and he brought this element, a high ideal, to the bulletin.

---

7. Comments in quotes are Miles', either witty or self-deprecating.

Sandhya Naidoo

Even in face to face encounters it was sometimes difficult to get a clear picture of the pioneers as, without exception, they were self-deprecating and Sandhya Naidoo was no exception. I found her straightforward and to the point. In 2004 she was still handsome with grey hair but it was not difficult to see her mid-1960s self. She was glamorous and fitted in with the "scene" of the time.[8] Like the other pioneers she was at the 1961 conference and agreed with Tim Miles that it had been a "stormy affair" and spoke of one educational psychologist being so angry that it was difficult to tell whether it was a man or woman as their "voice was so screechy". On being asked the reason for the anger she said it was educational psychologists mainly that weren't happy probably because medical men were handling the issue which the educational psychologists saw as part of education. Critchley in particular irritated them. The usual red-herring was that middle-class families were just finding excuses for their "thick" children. Naidoo was amazed at the conference and still was when we spoke but said "at least in 2004 people know what dyslexia means and there are 'believers and the non-believers'".

Naidoo became interested in reading when she did her education diploma in 1943 in Glasgow. A lecturer gave a series of talks on Schonnell "hot off the press at that time" and this sparked her attention.[9] Naidoo first taught in a secondary modern school and had a "lovely head teacher" who was kind but believed in probationary teachers being given a "baptism of fire" which in Naidoo's case was a class of 14-year-olds who "couldn't care a damn" and many of them had learning difficulties. The next year, Naidoo had eleven-year-olds and using the test from Schonnell's book she discovered four total non-readers. With the agreement of the school and their families she helped these children after school. Two of the four were twin girls and one burst into tears saying, "No one has cared about us before". These children fired Naidoo's imagination and started her work in the field.

---

8.   There are photographs of her in the publicity material of the Word Blind Centre.
9.   Sir Fred Joyce Schonnell was an Australian educationalist, and vice-chancellor of the University of Queensland from 1960 to 1969.

Naidoo taught for three years and then started a family but when the youngest was five she wanted to get back to work. She had an interest in left-handedness, having read a research report by Margaret Clark on the subject and she looked around with a view to working in this area. She spoke to Professor Philip Vernon who was working at the Institute of Education in London and Vernon said she should really work with his sister Maggie, but as she was working in Reading this would have been impossible for Naidoo who had three small children to cope with. Naidoo's MA was in neurologically-based psychology and the person she really wanted to work with was Oliver Zangwill. Vernon thought that was a splendid idea, Zangwill was in experimental psychology at Cambridge at the time and he agreed to take her on.

Naidoo's husband was working in Toronto, Canada as a psychiatrist; she thought about going with him but decided against the idea as he did not intend to stay for long. Time had gone by and her children were in boarding schools so it was possible for her to work in Cambridge and "keep terms" (a requirement of the university). As part of her MA, Naidoo studied children who were neither left-handed nor right-handed, ambidextrous, and she was allowed to work with five-year-old children in six or even schools in the Cheam area. She tested hundreds of children to pick out those who were ambilateral, and she matched these with norm groups of strongly left-handed or right-handed children. During this period Naidoo used a battery of tests relating to reading, spelling and speech, and also talked to mothers about their peri-natal history, and familial history which she was able to link to the test results.

It was an interesting study and it was following this work that she went to Cambridge. Later Zangwill wanted her to look at the possibility of left-handedness being to do with left brain injury and to carry on with her experimental groups in Surrey, but her husband came home and they moved house and family life got in the way. Naidoo had "kept her terms" and she went home to write up her thesis It never got finished. Naidoo said life was not the same when she was not living in Cambridge "so I am not a failed Phd just an uncompleted one". Sandhya Naidoo was also at the 1961 conference.

Maisie Holt

It is difficult to say whether Maisie Holt should be grouped with the pioneers but what is clear is that she was a driving force in getting the 1961 conference off the ground and instrumental in bringing to the public's attention the subject of word-blindness. Holt was from a prominent ship building family, was born in the first year of the twentieth century and lived to be 103. Her life's work covered psychology and education. Her obituary states that she gained a fellowship at Cambridge for her research into psychology and neurology and that she had a Frobel Institute qualification allowing her to teach and train children and teachers.[10] She was the head of a demonstration nursery school (probably Rachel Macmillan in London) and she lectured at London University.

Holt knew everyone and had her finger in many pies, for example she was involved in bringing radio into schools in 1935. Her obituary also refers to the invitations on the mantelpiece in her house in Cadogan Square that read "like a section of *Who's Who*". Like others of the pioneers she had a Second World War history where at Cambridge she helped Sir Frederick Bartlett in the selection of Royal Air Force bomber and fighter pilots. Still during the war, in 1942, she became the first educational psychologist on the Isle of Wight and kept a close connection with the island for the rest of her life.

She became interested in dyslexia through Dr E B Strauss who in 1938 was the head of psychology at Bart's.[11] Strauss frequently had children referred to him as did Holt, Critchley and White Franklin, with physical disorders such as asthma, stammering and stomach aches but who also could not read. Holt tells in her unpublished autobiography that Strauss insisted that she do something about this problem. She knew of Schonnell's work in mathematics and used his principle to isolate the child's literacy problems and then build up their learning and confidence through repetition.

---

10. *Isle of Wight County Press*, 31 October 2003.
11. Strauss had worked on the continent with Ernst Knetchmer and also with Sir Henry Head. These researchers all link together in their thoughts on the knotty subject of dyslexia.

Holt claimed that she realised that the research being undertaken in the USA and on the continent as well as in the UK was happening in isolation and that these researchers should be brought together to share their work. Also that this was the birth of the idea behind the 1961 conference into word-blindness. This position is disputed by other participants and they maintain that it was Alfred White Franklin that came up with the original idea. What is clear is that the conference stirred things up. Holt wrote:

> "[A]n unbelievable storm of abuse and opposition was aroused, chiefly from teachers and educational psychologists who seemed to feel that their ability in their own particular field was being critisised [sic] or attacked. Such is the conservatism of the English"[12]

Holt, as will be seen later, annoyed some of the others working with her on the Word Blind Committee and even Tim Miles was not complimentary about her. On asking Miles if Holt was a very flamboyant person as this is how she comes over on paper, Miles answered that "no" she was ordinary looking.

Holt was inundated with clients after the conference and "her list" caused a lot of trouble, but more of this later. She worked on at Bart's and in 1969 took on two trainees one of whom was probably Bevè Hornsby who, although not one of the Word Blind Centre pioneers, was important in the dyslexia movement.

---

12. Maisie Holt, "Dyslexia: A Historical Account with Special Reference to England", unpublished research notes, date unknown, courtesy of St Bartholomew's Hospital archive. http://woottonbridgeiow.org.uk/holtlm.php Holt according to contemporaneous witnesses was not an easy lady although many also praised her for the work she did with them or their children. Her unpublished autobiography is littered with spelling errors, many more than just typos and of a dyslexic nature so maybe Holt was an unidentified dyslexic and coped with the disorder unaided all her life.

From Percy to Peter

CHAPTER FOUR

The Conference

In 1960, the council of the Invalid Children's Aid Association (ICAA) discussed the possibility of holding a conference on word-blindness.[1] Children were presenting with physical health problems such as repeat abdominal pains or difficulty with breathing, but showing no diagnostic reason for their illnesses and many more, with emotional problems, were being referred to paediatricians and neurologists. The children were usually intelligent and the symptom they all had in common was an inability to read and/or spell.

The ICAA normally only worked with children with physical illnesses but, with an increasing number of reports coming from child guidance clinics, doctors, speech therapists, paediatricians and neurologists there was cause concern. An increasing number of its council were aware of word-blindness and considered it time to bring together the research and experience of those in the field from both the UK and abroad. The ICAA was prepared to be involved with this group of children because children with any physical or emotional illnesses in the early-1960s could be described as "invalids".

By 1961, in preparation for the conference, Alfred White Franklin was approaching people and centres that he knew by repute were working with word-blind children. One example was Tim Miles who became involved because of his paper "Two Cases of Developmental Aphasia" (1961) in which he described his work with two children with dyslexic problems. Another was a London County Council (LCC) delayed reading

---

1.   There are sometimes problems with dates. The Word Blind Committee was not always good with them, but—to avoid any confusion—they started planning in 1960, the first conference was held in 1961, and the report of the first conference appeared in April 1962.

clinic, the Tapp Street Clinic, visited by White Franklin and Maisie Holt. The children in this clinic had originally been referred to Moor House School because they had speech defects but were refused help because it was found that they also had dyslexia-type problems. White Franklin also called on his colleagues from the USA and researchers and teachers from Scandinavia. This of course was decades before the internet so to find speakers and delegates White Franklin had to rely on word of mouth and articles in learned journals

By the 1960s research into word-blindness was taking place in different centres in the UK and abroad, papers were being written and in some cases treatment centres had been started to help the children, but in the UK there was no cohesion and in the main the centres were working in isolation. The committee of the ICAA, although not a research unit, thought it important that this information should be voiced. An article was placed in *The Lancet* floating the idea and this was met with a positive response, but the committee was loath to use its funds to organize a conference as it was felt that donated money was for helping invalid children not running conferences. Alfred White Franklin set about raising the money and succeeded in persuading Miss Peggy Stymie and the Halley Stewart Trustees to underwrite the event. Bart's had a unit for word-blind children run by Maisie Holt and Alfred White Franklin worked there so it was understandable that Bart's agreed to house the conference.

The conference from today's perspective may seem out of date and the repetition of the material tedious but that is in hindsight. In 1961 it was all new. Gathering information was slow and disseminating it even slower. Added to the slow filtering of ideas was the massive prejudice there was between different professionals and their common attitudes to lay people, especially parents. The media has always liked a good story and they could see arguments brewing.

From the outset the conference was controversial. As a young psychology lecturer from the University of North Wales in Bangor, Tim Miles remembered it as "a stormy affair" as did Sandhya Naidoo. The first shock for the organizers was the number of people who wanted to attend. One hundred people were expected and when 350 seats had been booked a larger hall had to be found, even then would-be delegates had to be turned away. The second shock was the make-up of the audience: neurologists, paediatricians, medical officers of health, psychiatrists, psychologists, social workers, and various professors concerned with language and education, school teachers, parents and the media. Although most were there to learn about word-blindness some wanted to discuss all non-readers. The media had stirred up interest in "word-blindness" as by the early-1960s education had become "trendy". The colleges of education were growing year by year in size and research into all aspects of learning was burgeoning at a rate. However the idea that dyslexia was just a "middle-class disease" was the main reason for much media interest.

The day started with lectures to the whole conference and in the afternoon it split into smaller groups with short presentations on Theory, Diagnosis and Treatment, followed by discussions. The three groups reassembled at the end of the conference and each section was summed-up and there was a general discussion to finish off the day.

When reading the literature of the time, it is difficult to come to terms with the terminology: dullard, backward, retarded, all words used with impunity. The parents in the audience were referred to as "plain parents" meaning having little understanding of the subject; however this bit of terminology was later used by the parents to taunt the speakers and the plain parents answered back.

White Franklin gathered a wide group of speakers from the UK and abroad, and from different backgrounds; it was soon established that in the main the medical representatives and the parents were on one side supporting the proposition of word-blindness and the teachers and educational psychologists were the dissenters. As seen in a previous chapter, the early researchers were usually not educationalists and it was apparent at the conference how angry the educational psychologists were over the whole concept of dyslexia.

The morning

In welcoming the conference in the spirit of the time, Alfred White Franklin read a message of support from the patron of the ICAA, Princess

Margaret and he explained why it had taken over a year to get the conference off the ground. The first speaker was Dr Rosewell Gallagher, a well-known American, who had started as a school medical officer and was a friend of Samuel Orton, so he was well-versed in word-blindness. In 1961 he was a specialist in the new field of adolescence; teenagers had not been taken seriously prior to the Second World War, so he was seen as an innovator.

Gallagher set the scene by giving a brief history of word-blindness, the symptoms and the likelihood of the condition being inherited. He illustrated word-blindness by describing bizarre spelling, reversal of letters and changeable handwriting and he noted that the word-blind muddled words when reading and often added syllables. Like his predecessors in the field he had found that the word-blind were often of average or above average intelligence and some were good at mathematics. He felt that if there was any doubt as to diagnosis a family history of the condition would usually clinch the matter. He stressed that the child/adult should be carefully examined and an in-depth history of the patient and their family should be taken. He advised the audience on teaching methods he thought best-suited the word-blind, feeling prevention was better than cure. Prior to the child starting school a carefully observed history would show the more obvious symptoms of word-blindness, late talking, right left confusion and a family history of reading and spelling difficulties would alert the school to possible learning problems; and the child should then be put on a phonic reading programme from the beginning. Parents listening to Dr Gallagher must have been excited to hear their children described so accurately and have agreed vehemently with the speaker as to prevention being better than cure.

As the different lectures were given the audience became aware of the similarity of the content from each speaker. They all stated that the children in question were not generally deficient in intelligence or backward, nor had defective vision or hearing. Neither did they have brain damage due to injury or infection before or at the time of birth, or in early life. The children did not lack the developmental part of the brain, nor did they have identifiable emotional disturbance or lack education but all had problems with literacy.

Having looked at an American model the conference then moved to Denmark. Ingrid Riis-Vestergaard described the history of the dyslexic movement in that country. Danish state education assisted all children who were backward in reading but also recognised the syndrome of word-blindness. As well as the state system was a privately run institution started by Edith Norrie. Originally the state system and Edith Norrie Institute were run separately, but unlike in the UK there was never any animosity between the two and later the Norrie Institute was funded by state grants. The institute catered for a wide group of people, severely handicapped word-blind children, adults having problems with literacy in the workplace and children who were struggling with mild forms of word-blindness. The more severely handicapped children were taken out of school and taught full-time, while those with minor problems were taught on a part-time basis. Emphasis was placed on the student being made to feel comfortable and thereby building on their confidence and this was seen as vital a component as the teaching.

From Denmark the conference then moved to France, Madame de Séchelle's work on word-blindness was based around language disorders and her methods dated back to 1926 when the work was first undertaken by Madame Borel-Maisonny in Paris. The latter had soon discovered that some of the children with language disorders also found it difficult to learn to read and spell.

Madame de Séchelle gave a detailed explanation of the complicated nature of learning to read, but pointed out that the majority of children learn with no particular effort. She spoke of the many research groups attempting to discover the cause of word-blindness, but she felt that researchers should not rush to think they had found the answer. The French team were interested in the treatment of word-blindness. By finding the individual child's difficulty in the acquisition of literacy it was then possible plan a programme specifically to help them. Her programme was based on gesture and relied on establishing visual images of the letter that the child had problems retaining. She hastened to add that the programme was in its infancy and was so far only happening in hospitals, but that the results were looking favourable, and she asked the audience to view her exhibition to learn more of the project.

Professor Patrick Meredith concluded the morning lectures and his was probably the most difficult and thought-provoking of all those so far. He was an Emeritus Professor of Psychophysics at the University of Leeds specialising in visual education, psychology and mathematics. Professor Meredith, like the previous speakers, introduced his lecture with a brief survey of the history of word-blindness. He explained that, in his opinion, word-blindness or specific developmental dyslexia occurred for a variety of reasons, congenital, developmental, or neurological, or later in life as the result of an accident, all leading to a delay in the acquisition of literacy, and the necessity for special education, or in the case of acquired dyslexia, re-education.

Professor Meredith felt the complexity of the subject was due to each client/patient being an individual with differing symptoms. By definition the whole area of dyslexia was complex because the syndrome covered the working of the brain, and as a result language, behaviour and education. The only aspect the children/adults had in common was a need to find a way of coping with their handicap. Meredith saw this as the glue holding together all the practitioners: doctors, therapists, teachers and parents, and not least the client/patient.

"Obviously the brain is the crux of the matter but equally obviously our present picture of the brain is immensely confused." [2]

In charting the history of brain research, he moved from the simplistic view of each function, such as speech being located in one particular area of the brain, to the more recent complex discoveries of neurological interconnections. He looked forward to the day when researchers would be able to find the connections between the mind and the body.

Meredith's lecture must have been baffling to some members of the audience. At times it appeared to only be directed at those researching into reading difficulties. He recommended that research on reading should be collected and codified: "the need for an atlas". Meredith emphasised that until it was possible to see and understand the workings of the

2.   Conference report published April 1962, p. 29.

brain it was a matter of "not dealing with an established fact but with a belief."[3] As the audience was so diverse only some would have totally understood Meredith's lecture. His examples of individual differences were intricate and difficult but others of his audience would have appreciated his findings. He talked of the complexities encountered by the brain when faced with a single word, and the interconnections needed to make sense of such a word. As an example he spoke of research that showed that even when injured the brain could work around a problem. He used the comparison of a city that still functioned even when a bomb had exploded in a part of it.[4] Professor Meredith had come to the conclusion that just as a word might have several meanings or could be used in different contexts, the recognition and meaning of a word did not reside in one place in the brain. His opinion was that "storage" was copied into different areas; he used the example of keeping documents safe in wartime by copying them and placing the copies in different locations:

"[A] single brain-word is then a phase of the brain process rather than a local occurrence".[5]

At the conclusion of his lecture he appeared torn between wanting a working set of norms but also seeing that this was impossible. He wanted to accept some of the findings of the past but saw the necessity of building on them. Because of the density of the terminology and the ideas put forward it is possible to imagine just how confused some of his audience may have been, but also how stimulated and excited they were by his exploration and enlightenment.

At this point the conference broke for lunch, how fascinating to have been able to eavesdrop on some of the conversations. In the afternoon arguments were to rage, and parents were going to stand up and make their feelings heard. The different groups got together and gave one another courage to speak up and make their mark and how

---

3.   Ibid, p. 33.
4.   We forget how close 1961 was to the Second World War. Bombs and fighting were fresh in the memories of many.
5.   "Word-blindness of Specific Developmental Dyslexia", ibid, p. 34.

gratifying subsequently to find their thoughts written up in the conference proceedings.

The afternoon

In the afternoon the three sections, theory, diagnosis and treatment ran in parallel. The theory session started with Macdonald Critchley, a neurologist, who was famous in many areas of neurology as well as dyslexia and unlike some of the other speakers had a wealth of practical experience of working with dyslexic children.[6] He had been working with dyslexics since the 1920s and understood the "soft symptoms" of it. His description of the condition must have comforted many worried parents. He spoke of the child being able to list by rote the days of the week or the months of the year, but being unable to place accurately and in context a day or a month if not within the list. Among other soft symptoms was an inability to tap out rhythms, remember colours, and what he referred to as a "strange disability" of being unable to read facial expressions. He disagreed with other researchers as to a dyslexic's abilities with arithmetic, he felt that many did not grasp the concepts of multiplication, division, etc.

Referring to the original writings of Hinshelwood, Critchley was interested in comparing the problems associated with aphasia experienced by brain damaged adults but he did not identify acquired aphasia with developmental dyslexia. He considered that although speech delay was seen in young dyslexic children, and that in some cases this went on longer than would be expected, this should not be compared to adult aphasia.[7] He concluded that when the soft symptoms were found in adults they were the result of lesions in the brain and this wasn't so with children. Critchley observed that the soft symptoms experienced by the young child were usually overcome by the onset of adolescence, hence the term "late developer".

---

6.   Critchley mainly used the term "dyslexia" not "word-blind".
7.   Muddled words and phrases are common in young children, dyslexic youngsters carry on with these errors until they are taught out and in some this can be into adulthood. Eileen Simpson an eminent dyslexic writes in her autobiography, *Reversals*, 1991, Noonday Press, of "feathers'" on a tree when she meant "leaves".

Each of the presentations on theory was followed by a discussion session and Professor Meredith chaired the Critchley discussion. One of the main debates to unfold throughout the afternoon was the definition and description of the condition called word-blindness. An example which would leave a twenty-first century audience gasping was a speech therapist from St Bart's who suggested to Dr Critchley that he should use the American term "alogia" instead of aphasia to describe the "speech of the mentally defective". Other questions were asked about symptoms and corresponding ages and then one speaker, a teacher from a special school, suggested that Dr Critchley was talking about "sub-normal children". Dr Critchley quickly countered this by saying:

> "I am assuming of course, that intelligence tests have already been done and that subnormality has been eliminated."

Professor Meredith, in kindly fashion, finished the discussion by suggesting that if parents were made more aware of the soft symptoms they might realise sooner that their child was dyslexic and not just clumsy.

Mr D P Shankweiler spoke as part of the Theory Group. He was from the National Institute of Mental Health in America and like Dr Critchley found it worthwhile to look at the symptoms shown by the acquired dyslexic but he felt that "specific dyslexia" could be the result of minor brain damage. Later in the discussion session Dr Critchley disagreed with Shankweiler and he claimed that the evidence of genetics was now so strong that this ruled out brain damage as a cause, though obviously it could also be a contributory factor.

Mr Shankweiler was interested to know why after 60 years of research there were still more politically controversial discussions than hard facts about the cause of dyslexia. He felt that one of the reasons for this was that the questions asked were not specific enough and although the act of questioning was a difficult business it was possible. Mr Shankweiler thought researchers should look carefully at dyslexic children's speech. He considered that as most dyslexic children had good verbal skills, as Hinshelwood and Morgan had noted the disability had always been seen as a reading problem. Like others Shankweiler had looked at differences in reading techniques exhibited by the dyslexic, for example how individual letter sounds could be recognised but not when blended to make words. He was interested in Orton's 1925 work on reversal and felt that spatial awareness was of great significance as this affected copying, clock reading and laterality. Like Dr Critchley he had observed spatial awareness problems mainly in young dyslexics, but he thought the problem often persisted into adolescence. Shankweiler's aim was to research precisely and to build blocks of knowledge to enable training programmes to be designed to help the children overcome their particular difficulties. Following this session, chaired by Professor Meredith, was a discussion amongst researchers. In the audience was Professor Zangwill,[8] who was aware of Shankweiler's and Critchley's research. He concluded that, as others had said, the subject of dyslexia covered many areas of expertise: neurology, psychology, education and remedial work. He hoped that the conference would be able to pull all disciplines together and to coordinate research into training.

A psychiatrist, Dr Booth drew attention to how unhappy dyslexic children were. He felt that a lot of effort and experience was being wasted because people like him were working with children but did not have the time or the expertise to gather results or undertake any research. Professor Meredith completely agreed with Booth and added examples of his own. He talked of filing cabinets full of data and a need for improved record keeping. He asked that the conference should recommend to the Medical Research Council that money should be allocated for systematic research. Professor Zangwill however warned that a lot of workers in the field would rather money was spent on the diagnosis and teaching of affected children. He did think that pooling information would be as beneficial as would research, but felt that this should be undertaken by people actively working with children/adults and that the results of the research should be mirrored in the remedial teaching methods.

Professor Meredith asked for the opinion of any teachers in the audience. One teacher said he thought the majority of teachers would just consider dyslexic children as dull, and another teacher and an educational

---

8.   Oliver Zangwill pops up throughout this history. For a while he was on the Word Blind Committee and he influenced and supported both Naidoo and Miles.

psychologist agreed saying that a recent survey of headteachers had shown that they had not even heard of the condition. Two parents joined in and said that their children were not understood and were called lazy by their teachers. Professor Meredith agreed that there was widespread ignorance of the subject of dyslexia.

One of the teachers emphasised that she and her colleagues were trying to get help for all children with reading difficulties and this theme re-occurred in other discussion groups. If money was spent on dyslexic children it would not be spent on other children with reading problems. Critchley felt that the fault lay with the Ministry of Education who until the early-1960s had not recognised the condition of dyslexia.

Meredith brought the session to a close by saying:

> "This is something so subtle that only a very sensitive teacher can watch for
> the signs of readiness or resistance and try to follow along at the child's own
> possibly irregular pace." [9]

There were two presentations on the diagnosis of dyslexia and it is possible that in retrospect White Franklin wished he had chosen other speakers. The first, Mr C Worster-Drought was an experienced assessor and had in twelve years seen 75 cases of dyslexia, however the children he worked with were primarily those with speech disorders and as such it was difficult for the assessor to ascertain the major reason behind a child not reading. Worster-Drought stated that all the dyslexic children he had seen were of average or above average intelligence with similar problems as seen by the other speakers. He felt it was possible that dyslexic children were more likely to have speech defects than non-dyslexic children.

The second speaker was Margaret Reingold and she considered dyslexia to be a condition purely of poor literacy, although as her lecture unfolded she eluded to the same soft signs Critchley had described. As the title of her lecture was "Diagnosis" Reingold gave the audience a run-down of what an assessor should be looking for. She considered it quite possible for a young dyslexic child to pass unnoticed through nursery

---

9.   "Word-blindness of Specific Developmental Dyslexia", ibid, p. 63.

and even the first years at primary school without there being particular problems. Only when faced with more advanced reading would the child slip behind and show signs of distress. Parents must have experienced this scenario. At this point the educational psychologist would be called in and Reingold advised questioning the parents as to any family history of reading problems. She advised continuing with a closer examination of the child's early development. Parents would frequently remember the child's difficulties tying bows, distinguishing left from right, and learning to tell the time. Whilst taking the child's history it was also possible to establish the nature of the child's home life and the support that might be available.

Dangerously, Margaret Reingold stated that she could assess whether the child was of average intelligence just by talking to them. This statement later came in for much criticism from the educational psychologists present. Continuing with her subject she advocated using a checklist from which she would build a picture of the child's ability. She, like Critchley, felt developmental dyslexics had difficulties with arithmetic and in her experience with distinguishing between plus and minus signs and so on. The final section of her assessment process was spent in testing laterality and looking in some detail at the child's ability to tie a bow and open doors. She felt that intelligence tests could be used, but that this was probably only necessary when carrying out research. She concluded each session with a child by allowing time for free drawing, and felt she could judge the child from the drawings.

Sir Wilfred Sheldon chaired the discussion group for this session, and he was interested in the opinions of the teachers. He probably sensed danger as the researchers wished only to discuss elements of diagnosis; they were particularly interested in laterality, the main opinion being that an inability to read and cross-laterality ran parallel but that the cross-laterality was not a causal factor in reading difficulty. Several educational psychologists argued against the individual tests used by the two speakers in their diagnosis. An educational psychologist got heated about the lack of norms in some of the tests used by the speakers, and went on to argue against all of the symptoms cited. His argument was that, among the general population, few children could recite the alphabet which reflected the growing trend of teaching reading as a whole word process, usually called "look and say". A paediatrician jumped in and said the educational psychologist was contradicting himself. The discussion ended with a speaker ascertaining that there was so much resistance to the whole concept of dyslexia because the antagonists had just not seen the condition.

To counter the negative arguments was the experiences of several teachers and educational psychologists who had worked with dyslexic children. An educational psychologist stated that he at first had been completely against the whole concept of dyslexia but was now in agreement. He had seen several children of around nine-years-of-age who had a good verbal IQ of 120 but with performance IQs of 100, and that he felt this was a reflection of "a minimal neurological disorder". What worried him most was how unhappy these children were ("He is a bag of nerves") and he asked if it was reasonable to assume that this child was dyslexic as he couldn't see any reason for them not reading. Helen Arkell explained how a child reading aloud often could not tell what they had read because they were concentrating so hard on the process of reading. She claimed the lack of attentiveness in the young adult was due to their falling behind with their studies and loosing heart, and Dr Worster-Drought agreed that lack of concentration could be an emotional problem.

The third and last set of presentations were on "training" and given by J C Daniels, Maisie Holt and Tim Miles, all three educational psychologists and who were teaching children as well as assessing them.

Dr Daniels was hugely anti the whole concept of dyslexia, rubbishing the work of the early researchers, e.g. Hinshelwood and Morgan. He loathed the idea that the symptoms seen in the adult acquired dyslexic were similar to those seen in the developmental dyslexic. He made it plain that he was of the opinion that the researchers in this area thought that dyslexic children could not be taught and that by giving children the label "dyslexic" or "word-blind" teachers would give up on the child and they would be left untaught.

Daniels was researching into reading difficulties and among other works he was the joint author of a reading test and reading scheme, which he mentioned often in his lecture. From his explanation of the work he had undertaken with groups of non-readers he had taught them well and, when faced with children who with normal remediation had not responded, had analysed their problems and come up with methods that had worked. On the day of the conference he was an angry man, it sounded as though he should have been an advocate for the emergent dyslexia movement but he saw it as a threat.

As seen, Maisie Holt had been part of the team setting up the conference on word-blindness and perhaps found it difficult to follow Dr Daniels. In her introduction she spoke of setting up the centre at Bart's. Dr Eric Strauss recognising the condition of dyslexia insisted that the children were to be helped. Because of his insistence Holt had by the time of the conference worked with 200 children, although this had not been an easy task. Dr Strauss had also felt that the very treatment had a therapeutic effect on the children whatever they were taught. No doubt this was true but it can't have helped the argument when many in the audience were looking for stringent research and formal treatment.

Holt's talk continued in a rather vague manner until it came to the account of the testing undertaken with the children, which was rigidly building a solid educational profile. When it came to teaching programmes, like many of the other speakers she felt that phonic methods were more effective than "look and say", but she was a bit hazy when it came to what actually was taught. Holt felt strongly that no two children were the same. She had success with the children she worked with, always using multi-sensory teaching methods.

The final speaker in this group was Tim Miles and his lecture was based on the work that he had been undertaking in Bangor with two children suffering from developmental dyslexia. From a research perspective he recognised that two was not an adequate sample, but considered that the amount of detail he had gathered made up for the lack of numbers. He had been careful to screen for any other causes of reading problems: health, IQ or emotional state. He had received considerable support from the children's parents and was able to teach them individually and on a regular basis. Miles felt that the term dyslexia covered "a family of disabilities",[10] and that the methods he used with the children were appropriate to all "members of the family". His research showed that dyslexics do not process symbols in the same way as non-dyslexics. He explained that the average reader hears a sound and goes straight to "its symbolic visual representation", i.e. a letter, whereas the dyslexic first hears a sound and then has to convert the symbol through the movements made by the mouth and tongue, i.e. speech into a visual symbol or letter. Furthermore the dyslexic did not always automatically blend together sounds to make a word. Miles discovered on showing his subjects' written work to a specialist in speech education that they were spelling phonetically and with obvious signs of intelligence. He decided to use these skills to teach the children and this is why he called his technique the "phonetic cues" method.[11] He willingly admitted that his idea was not original, and that even if his audience disregarded the term dyslexia the method worked because it was theoretically sound. Miles believed that his techniques were effective and that this belief was important in teaching. He suggested that as his methods had been successful with two children it was worth pursuing the techniques with larger groups

Dr T T S Ingram chaired the discussion that followed the last theory session and he attempted to undo some of the knots that had formed concerning definitions of dyslexia. He emphasised again that in an attempt to clarify definitions the conference was discussing children with a particular set of problems and although other difficulties arose because of their disability they were secondary to the main theme of the day. Of course this was all very well but the symptoms of dyslexia were varied and carried different weights of disability for different children that made definitions almost impossible. On reading the report it appears Ingram was also trying to take the sting out of the arguments between the believers in the concept of dyslexia and the others that saw it as an excuse.

No sooner had Dr Ingram finished speaking than Mr Walbridge, an educational psychologist, spoke (and one senses the irritation) of the amount of work already happening in the field. He had been working with children with reading problems since 1942 and spoke in some detail

---

10. Words in quotes from the transcript of the conference.
11. Whether Miles was aware that he was using Mason's technique is unclear.

of the need for diagnosis. By this presumably he meant exactly diagnosing a child's difficulties. He went on the echo Joyce Morris' argument
that some children just didn't have the tools to attack reading. He was
particularly concerned with "orientation", a subject which Patrick Meredith went on to write a book about, *Dyslexia and the Individual.*

At this point up popped a parent intent on receiving advice on how
to help his child, an eleven-year-old boy with an IQ of 142 (he had been
assessed by Dr Critchley at Queen's Square) with a reading age of 5.5
years. The conference swung from highly technical discussions of current research to hands on advice for worried parents. Miles and Daniels
immediately stepped in with helpful practical ideas to help the boy. The
parents proceeded to take centre stage; they must have still been smart-
ing from the "plain parent" description as they use this title repeatedly.
Mrs Davie of London:

> "As a plain parent, as we were designated this morning, I am almost too
> scared to speak in front of any of you, quite literally, because mostly anything
> I say on it is dismissed as absolute nonsense. Parents usually know least of
> all, unfortunately."[12]

Mrs Davie must have spoken for so many parents who were battling
for help for their children:

> "And the thing that depresses me so much that I could weep, is the fact that
> the people in education have said to me, he could do it if he wanted to, and
> I as a humble and obviously very ignorant parent, am quite convinced he
> couldn't do it if he wanted to."[13]

Maisie Holt must have heard these stories from the hundreds of parents she had seen at Bart's and the first inkling of her ambition for a
teaching training centre is voiced in her concern for Mrs Davie. Mr Jack
Jones (Central Office of Information) reminded the conference that it
was the law since 1944 that every child should be taught according to

---

12. Conference report, p. 109.
13. Ibid.

their needs. Mrs Christie (Devon) encouraged her fellow parents to keep fighting and not to give up. She had fought and got her child over the first "hump" as the initial learning to read had become known, what worried her was how were their capable children to get through all the examinations that were on the road to an adequate career.

The Association for Parents of Word-blind Children was born at the conference. Mrs Le Grice (St Albans):

> "Just one last thing. Would it be possible for all puzzled parents to form the sort of *Word-Blind Anonymous* organisation, by which we could keep in touch, and perhaps have guidance from people who have spoken today, and others who have made a detailed study of the problem."[14]

Miles stands out in the discussion as the evangelist for the parents and the children and he brought the arguing and debating to a close by forcefully encouraging the parents not to give in or think that they were ignorant as in his opinion they knew best what was wrong with their children. Many decades later he was still laughing at the effect the parents had and what an important contribution they made at the conference. Ingram rounded off this session by saying:

> "I would particularly like to say how pleased we were to hear the views of parents so well expressed. They have been terribly useful."[15]

The summing-up

The first conference was nearly over and White Franklin brought the groups together for a summing-up and a last Q&A session and did the sparks fly? Looking at the different viewpoints from the distance of many decades it is easy to see why there were misunderstandings and illogical standpoints. It is difficult in the twenty-first century with the internet to understand why the different protagonists did not see the others' points of view but they didn't have our present day access to information. Professor

---

14.　Ibid, p. 112.
15.　Ibid, p. 114.

Meredith summing-up session-one came to this conclusion without the aid of the internet. He felt what was needed was more research and that there should be "improved standardisation of forms, and the pooling of information." He saw the need for more remedial teachers and for the Ministry of Education to be persuaded of the reality of dyslexia.

Sir Wilfred Sheldon reporting on session two wittily knitted together the diagnostic arguments and how confusing they were. He understood that in looking for dyslexia it was helpful to rule out other causal conditions for non-reading be they physical or emotional. Interestingly he underlined the fact that a child with other disabilities could also be dyslexic and that the researchers were excluding other problems only to make their research clearer; this apparently sensible concept was used later as a weapon against the dyslexic movement time and again.

> "It was recognised that this condition can occur in children who have hearing difficulties, difficulties of vision, or emotional disturbances. That was to say, the presence of these other disorders wouldn't exclude the child from having developmental dyslexia, but that in order to make progress in this condition, one should, in the first place, limit oneself to children who had clear-cut cases of dyslexia without these associated phenomena."[16]

Sheldon reported the discussions on dominance and laterality which were the cornerstone of the research in the USA but were not considered so important by UK researchers. He finished by also emphasising how many children in London could not read; one per cent and that it was ten per cent in approved schools.

Professor Meredith reported on the third-session, "Treatment", and he merely summed-up what the three speakers had said. Interestingly he side-stepped the controversy and the parents' contributions. Perhaps as a result Alfred White Franklin asked a parent to start off the final Q&A session. Firstly however he asked the assembly what they should do next. The ICAA was not an academic institution and what they really wanted

---

16.   Ibid, p. 118.

to do was help "invalid" children. White Franklin asked for help in this dilemma, where next?

White Franklin was cunning in his choice of parent to start the final act of the conference. Mr Travers Healey was a journalist so was used to communicating. He said he felt like an evangelist at a revivalist meeting and like all evangelists he gave the assembly a personal story. The oldest of his five children, a boy, was not doing well at school although he was bright, and probably because he was bright his father thought he was just not trying hard enough to learn to read. Their previously happy home was disrupted by this now difficult stroppy child and not only at home but also at school where he was becoming anti-social. The school were concerned and persuaded Mr Travers Healey to allow the boy to be seen by a psychologist at Bart's. As a result of his assessment and presumably some teaching young Master Travers Healey was by the time of the conference doing well, so well that although he still made many errors he was happy and was reading books that interested him and was writing "voluminously". In true evangelical fashion Travers Healey then admitted that he too couldn't spell and that neither could his father.

Travers Healey's clarion call was to start an association, not anonymous but noisy, trumpeting success stories like that of his son. He said the parents (19) were consumers and should use the propaganda of the consumer through the auspicious ICAA, very 1960s.

The Q&A session then got into full swing and again the arguments between the educational psychologists and those committed to the dyslexic movement really took off. One psychiatrist agreed that research should take place and that the child guidance centres should be the place for this. Others pointed out that the clinics were overloaded as it was and wouldn't have time for more commitments. Then one educational psychologist, Mr Walbridge, calling on Dr Daniels to back him up, said that those working with the ICAA should be aware of all the papers that had been written on the subject over the last 20 years and reviewed in the *British Journal of Educational Psychology*. White Franklin appeared amazed at the answer and called on Miles to comment:

"There is one brief point, I am surprised to hear about *The British Journal of Educational Psychology*, as I have done quite a lot of homework on it. I know of no article on dyslexia in it, but I shall be glad to be enlightened."[17]

This was probably the point in the conference when it was admitted by all parties that dyslexia existed but that many did not want to admit it. Mr Walbridge's answer to Miles was:

"Well, you will find many references are relevant in the *British Journal of Educational Psychology*. They don't call it dyslexia, of course, they call it various things. You have to treat for this."[18]

Alfred White Franklin became annoyed:

"We sound as though we are back at square one. I think you are really trying to have it both ways."

He had hoped that by bringing together experts on the subject of word-blindness that the conference would agree that there was a special group of children and that they should not be lumped together with all non-readers. This appeal got nowhere. The majority of the educational psychologists and psychiatrists where not prepared to admit to anything. Dr Daniels got so angry because he felt that to admit that a child was word-blind/dyslexic was backward thinking and would just place "a ball and chain" around the ankle of the child and with such a diagnosis teachers would give up and not bother to teach the child.

Next steps

This was 1961. The conference was in the prestigious surroundings of Bart's. One can imagine the room, high ceilings, polished wood floors, and it was stacked out with people. The men would have been dressed formally; White Franklin and Critchley always wore old-fashioned

---

17.   Ibid, p. 127.
18.   Ibid, p. 128.

consultants formal suits with waistcoats and probably watch chains across their chests. The other men would have been similarly attired. The women might have been a little less formal but even so it would have been "visiting London clothes", suits and court shoes. All of them by this time of day must have been hot under the collar, red in the face and blustering.

The argument went on with more and more reasons for not recognising the condition but Professor Meredith brought an end to the list of speakers who were against the whole concept. He suggested a scenario to the conference: if a remedial teacher was faced with two children, both of whom could not read, one had specific rather than general difficulties while the other all round learning problems, wouldn't the type of teaching for each child be different? The second child would eventually read but they would have to go "slow and steady" but this approach would not work with the first child. This seemed to hearten more parents and professionals who were brave enough to give examples of methods that had helped with word-blind children.

The conference ended as it began with Dr Roswell Gallagher. This mild-mannered Irish American was obviously amused by what he had seen and heard. He had been exposed to a lot of ideas and battles in his time.[19] He knew Orton intimately and from this lofty position he was not worried by the confusion or about names. He was sure that dyslexia existed, he had seen too many young people suffering from the disorder to have any doubts but the only thing of importance for him was that children and young people should be helped and taught. He saw that this also involved teaching the teachers which is what he was attempting to do in the USA and he saw the merits of an association for parents and suggested calling it "Can't read/Can't spell".

Before the very end Alfred White Franklin was urged to set up a body to train specialist teachers by Dr Daniels, to encourage the government to find more money for "remedial teachers" by Mr Shearn, and to ask the ICAA to make parents of dyslexic children aware of what facilities were available by Dr Berg. Armed with the requests White Franklin assured

---

19.   Gallagher lived on until he was 92, so almost spanning the whole of the twentieth century.

the meeting that he would take all their requests and ideas back to the executive committee of the ICAA and in true gentlemanly fashion he took that opportunity to thank all those who had organized the event. The transcript of the proceedings was published in 1962 and circulated mainly within the education world.

CHAPTER FIVE

Class, Madness and Charities

Class, madness and charities have played a part in the dyslexia movement. It was because of a doctor's concerns for Percy and similar children that the research started into word-blindness in children, and that in turn, though many decades later, led to the Word Blind Centre, supported by the Invalid Children's Aid Association (ICAA). In the 1960s the ICAA was a large and prestigious charity; Queen Elizabeth II was patron and Princess Margaret president.

State laws have existed to assist the poor and needy since the Reformation, the most famous being the Elizabethan Act of 1601 which legislated to house and protect the poor and needy. Charity was not easy to obtain nor bountiful, but provision was there by law. Local landowners and the householders of a parish were taxed, and a worthy elected to administer the funds. Prior to that it was mainly the established church that ministered to those in need and provided support to those unable to work. As part of this provision, education of the poor was always in the mix. The Reformation destroyed this welfare system and the 1601 poor laws acted as a counterbalance. However, within a community, charity was provided to supported individuals and/or groups of people in need. In essence where there is a want, usually a group of people will get together and raise funds or goods to help those in need. This concept is as active today as it has always been. In today's climate charities are an "add-on" because of the welfare state but prior to the mid-twentieth century state support was so limited that charities determined how much welfare took place, and this often covered education and medical help for those who could not afford it as seen, e.g. in the ragged schools movement.

One can't argue against charity. It is an integral part of most religions and a natural instinct of caring people. But charity has a sub-text, networking. Running a charity is all about a group of people getting together to raise money, services or goods but in so doing they gain enjoyment and individuals increase their network of contacts. The downside of this admirable pursuit is that those not involved in the charity are "on the outside". Charities can also be seen as part of the class structure; some charity committees are more prestigious than others and fundraising events can be lavish and exclusive. By definition charities are the "haves" giving to the "have nots" and "I don't want charity" was a heartfelt cry from many as it meant the recipient was at the bottom of the social pile.

People like Sir George Haynes are the epitome of the positive nature of charity. Sir George was born the son of railway worker and gained a BSc from Liverpool University in 1922. He worked the whole of his life in different charities and voluntary organizations for the good of others. He started as a teacher in Liverpool but soon moved to the National Council of Social Service (NCSS) which grew out of the charities born in the First World War. He and his family moved to London in 1936 and he worked there through the war helping with the problems thrown up by the blitz and evacuation. He was given a CBE in 1945 for his war efforts.

Sir George was heavily involved in setting up the Citizen's Advice Bureau through the NCSS and one of the main tasks was to translate official documents into plain English for the many in need of information. At the end of the Second World War, the NCSS produced several publications using experience and statistics obtained during the war, one of which was *Our Towns: A Close Up* which opened many people's eyes to the state of literacy in Britain. Sir George continued working in the field of social care and one of the committees he sat on was that of the ICAA which was why he gave the closing speech at the final conference of the Word Blind Centre, but more of that later.[1]

Allen Dowdeswell Graham, a clergyman, founded the ICAA in 1888 to help children who were ill, handicapped and poor. He wrote:

---

1.   See further *Oxford Dictionary of National Biography*, 2004, Oxford University Press.

"Poverty is bad enough, God knows, but the poor handicapped exist in a living hell. It's up to us to do something about it".[2]

Graham persuaded groups of volunteers to visit children who were ill or disabled and provide them with food, bedding and disability aids. The charity organized hospitalisation and placed children in convalescent homes. In 1891, Princess Mary of Teck (later Queen Mary) became the charity's patron. The ICAA soon moved from using volunteers to employing social workers to look after the children and needed money to carry out the work as well as volunteers to assist. "Homes of Recovery" were set up to cater for children suffering from tuberculosis and rheumatic heart disease. It seems that whenever a new need was discovered the ICAA was there to help and, after the introduction of the 1948 National Health Act, this did not change as the association saw its role as supporting parents to aid in the recovery of children. It was not surprising therefore that the ICAA should have been in the middle of the controversy concerning word-blindness, especially as Alfred White Franklin was active in the charity. From the beginning, the push to understand dyslexia and assist those suffering from it caused controversy as the group of children concerned were specific and odd. The dyslexic group worked with were of average intelligence and could not read so that to the uninitiated these children were either lazy or their parents were finding excuses for them.

For the ICAA, lack of funds was always a problem. In 1908 in the *British Medical Journal,* Warrington Haward and C W Fremantle wrote of the good works of the ICAA and how kind medical people were in their support, but that the association's funds were exhausted so could donations be sent. In the 1960s, as president, Princess Margaret actively supported the charity's work and she was a great asset. Much funding for prestigious charities in the 1960s, as now, was through social events and she led the social scene of the time. Amongst Arthur White Franklin's papers are newspaper cuttings and photographs of her including one of

2. Eleanor Davis Colley wrote about how Dowdeswell Graham set up the ICAA and Corinne Hogan (31 Aug 2018) wrote about her in an article on the ICAA: see https://www.rcseng.ac.uk/library-and-publications/library/blog/eleanor-davies-colley-and-the-invalid-childrens-aid-association/

her marriage to the Earl of Snowdon. Among the guests were the White Franklins. Princess Margaret was a guest of honour at a showing of *Anastasia* a popular conspiracy film about one of Margaret's Russian cousins who, in the film, did not die at the hands of the Russian revolutionaries but survived. She also took part incognito in an amateur production called *The Frog* at the Scala Theatre. The cast was made up of the "in" crowd and the programme gilt-edged, with advertisements for famous emporia, restaurants, literary events, newspapers and even bicycles. The events that the princess took part in were glittering affairs and she was at the centre of the London social scene. Charity events were and are worthwhile and raised much needed money but in the 1960s they were seen as middle-class activities, which further added to the perception of dyslexia as "the middle-class disease".

When I first heard of the "dyslexia" it was in fact attached to the term middle-class disease and it was understood that this epithet indicated that the middle-classes had made up a disorder to cover for their otherwise stupid children. Tim Miles and his colleagues at the University of North Wales worked on data obtained from the BCS70, a multi-disciplinary longitudinal study of 17,000 babies born between the 5th and 11th of April 1970 (estimated to be between 96–98 per cent of all births) and from this data proved that dyslexia was not confined to one socio-economic group. However the argument that dyslexia is a made up phenomena does not go away, and it may be because of deep-rooted and complex attitudes to intelligence and class.

It is fascinating to observe the antagonism that the syndrome has raised amongst some professionals and a wide range of individuals. One clue to this enmity may again be attributed to the class system in England and Wales and to fear of the unknown, in particular madness. Class, madness and charities tend to be mixed together in this story but madness in its broadest sense perhaps can stand alone, especially as for some at the time madness and intelligence were closely linked. The two World Wars and especially the Second World War had exposed the lack of education amongst huge groups of men; the classes had been mixed together in a way not heard of before and soldiers coming back from war were not willing to accept the old class order. As a direct result, in teacher training colleges in the mid-1960s it was politically incorrect to presume intelligence had anything to do with class. Intelligence testing was frowned upon by many educators; the argument was that such tests set children in a ridged inescapable framework, even checklists were forbidden. A joke was passed about that a teacher was given a list of numbers attached to the names of her new class and she presumed they were their IQ results and treated the children accordingly. At the end of the year she tested the children and found they conformed to the original numbers. It was only at this point that she discovered the numbers were in fact cloakroom peg numbers; a silly joke but indicative of the atmosphere at the time. The "checkist" theory held more water as if the teacher worked to one it was only human nature to feel that if the child had completed the list the teacher had done their job.

The big question argued over endlessly was "nature or nurture", and this is probably an argument still raging in educational establishments. The followers of Anna Freud and Melanie Klein had altered the face of post-war education by introducing the concept of the child's emotional state affecting educational achievement, i.e. nurture over nature. They, along with John Bowlby, did much to change the lives of children for the better. Both Klein and Freud were interested in children's fantasy worlds, how their minds worked, and used play as a way of understanding this. Bowlby, who was to some extent at odds with both psychoanalysts, believed that young children were affected by their early relationship to their significant adult, usually their mother. The war had of course opened-up an amazing arena for research into children who were removed from an important adult carer, again usually the mother. Europe was awash with children who had been treated in appalling ways and even in Britain those who had been evacuated to escape the worst effects of the bombings suffered the effects of separation; research in the 1940s and 1950s considered the results of these separations and whether children's abilities to learn and become socialised were affected. The Tavistock Clinic in London was central to much of this work; the thinking rarely allowed for neurological reasons for difficulties with literacy but blamed all such problems on the child's emotional state.

Tim Miles worked at the Tavistock Clinic in the early-1960s. He was not surprised that parents who presented at the clinic were worried about their children, and thought it perfectly normal that they would be concerned, if not stressed, that their children couldn't read. In retrospect, Miles considers that "Somehow they got the direction of causality wrong"[3] by moving away from seeing the problem as a physical one to thinking of it as emotional. As a result of his work at the Tavistock Miles, in consultation with Bowlby, came to the conclusion that some children were non-readers not through emotional upset within the family and he was able to reassure parents that it was not their fault that their child was dyslexic; and that they had not caused the dyslexia by anything they had done. Miles was a great believer in using commonsense guidance in his work. However he admired the work done by the Tavistock in that it took family relationships seriously at a time when most of the psychological world was concentrating on experimentation on rats and the like. He agreed with the Tavistock's attitude that a dyslexic child affected the whole family, and the stress and worry caused could arguably be as important as the problems with literacy being experienced by the child.

At the Tavistock, Miles saw cases of dyslexia and he was open in his opinions as to why the children were not reading. This caused quite a row, as the die hard Kleinians would have none of it. One case in particular interested Miles where there appeared to be no difficulties with the family dynamics. John Bowlby thought it could be a case of minor organic brain damage. Miles listened with admiration to Bowlby defending his view to his colleagues although Miles considered the child to have word-blindness (the diagnosis of which incidentally came as a great relief to the boy's parents).

The thinkers and researchers into dyslexia (still called word-blindness) in the late-1950s and early-1960s found them in an educational world that held wide-ranging views about nature verses nurture, the emotional state of the child and family, opinions on intelligence testing, in fact all testing. IQ testing and heredity were not part of general thinking. Macdonald Critchley and Arthur White Franklin had been working since

---

3.   Interview Two, August 27th 2002, University of North Wales, Bangor, T Miles and J Beard.

the 1950s with children at London hospitals. They linked these children with the pre-war findings of the early researchers into word-blindness, but to do so it was necessary to test them: to look at their basic intelligence, their levels of literacy and numeracy, and this approach fell foul of mainstream educationalist thinking of the time.

But does the whole concept of dyslexia go deeper than this? So many educationalist and journalists have been ferocious in their denunciation of it. Parents have been, and still are, scared of their child being labelled "dyslexic" as if it will make the child a pariah. Is there an underlying concern causing these reactions? The literature on word-blindness pre-1970 often referred to "idiots" and "imbeciles" when mentioning children who had not learnt to read. In the state schools such children were referred to child guidance clinics.

In law, idiots, lunatics and imbeciles were not considered capable of handling their lives and laws to organize such people go back to the thirteenth century, and these were still clearly in the minds of many as late as the 1960s. Ninetieth century literature is full of references to people being "put away" in asylums. Educationalists of the time stated that children shouldn't be labelled. For some the label was not a problem but for others it was distressing. I was first alerted to why parents could be nervous of labelling when talking to parents who had, in the 1970s, had their daughter "statemented"[4] and they were worried that they would lose rights over their child and that she might be sent to a school that they did not consider suitable for her. How many children did child guidance clinics send to special schools without the agreement of their parents?

As if this was not enough to horrify parents of otherwise normal children, Sir Cyril Burt must have sent shivers down their spines. In an article by Burt written in 1966 he rants about the term dyslexia; much of what he writes mirrors the findings of the dyslexia movement but he was adamant that there was not a specific condition. In the same article he more worryingly wrote:

4.   See *Chapter One.*

"Most backward readers are found in the lower manual classes: and here there is often little incentive or opportunity for reading during leisure hours; the family's vocabulary is extremely limited; and the pronunciation is far removed from that assumed by the conventional methods."[5]

Burt's understanding of limited vocabulary and reading is one thing but his sweeping assumption that "most backward readers are found in the lower manual classes" is another. Perhaps this is less surprising when understanding that although Burt was a psychologist he was also a eugenicist. His field of research was in intelligence testing and he had come under the influence of Sir Francis Galton who invented eugenics believing that there was a direct correlation between intelligence and class.

Galton's model of society had those of independent or professional means at one end of a scale and criminals and undesirables at the other. Eugenicists believed that defects in society could be bred out, but only if there was no inter-breeding between the classes. In extreme cases Galton believed in enforced sterilisation for those suffering from mental or physical defects. Eugenics of course became the excuse of the Nazis to support the extermination of Jews, gypsies, homosexuals, the disabled and other minorities they happened to disapprove of. Burt did not go to these extremes but he and his colleagues felt that the lower classes were not only less intelligent, they were also more fertile and this combination, if allowed to mix, would soon lower the overall intelligence of the population. Scarily, others who believed in this movement consisted of famous names such as John Maynard Keynes, George Bernard Shaw, H G Wells and even Winston Churchill. In Britain the eugenicists were referred to as "positive" rather than "negative" eugenicists, the negative model being the one used under the Nazis.

The Eugenics Society in England was powerful and helped to have the Mental Deficiency Act of 1913 passed which saw "defective children" sent to special schools. These children were termed "feebleminded" and Burt, who was now the chief psychologist for the London County Council (LCC), designed and constructed tests to pick out such children. He had

5. "Counterblast to Dyslexia Disability in Reading", *Association of Educational Psychologist's Newsletter*, 1966, No. 5, Sir Cyril Burt's Page, p. 2.

early in his career undertaken research which he said proved that intelligence directly related to class and he firmly believed this to the end of his working life. It begins to make more sense as to why ordinary families would be worried about their child being labelled dyslexic and why the hereditary issue was not comforting. It is obvious after reading accounts of special schools that some children referred to as mentally deficient, retarded or feeble-minded were in fact dyslexic. But who wanted those labels attached to their bright, talkative young sons or daughters?

Why the "middle-class disease" label? This is more difficult but it must revolve around the general animosity towards class in Britain. If people like Burt really believed that intelligence was a top down issue, where did this leave the "respectable working-class", which is what Galton called the large group found slap bang in the middle of his model of society? He knew they were hugely useful to society but equally thought it would water down the intelligence gene pool if they interbred with those at the top of the tree. This was not a new philosophy as seen earlier. In the late-1940s, the "respectable working class" was coming home from fighting for King and country and they must have been appalled by Burt's theories. Middle-class parents finding an excuse for their children not being able to read would be open to ridicule. Equally it was brave parents who fought for their children to receive the type of education that they needed in the climate of the 1960s.

The comments made in the press had a lasting impression on those working at the Word Blind Centre as they were still talking about it decades later, so the parents must have been equally upset. Many of the parents of dyslexic children at the end of the nineteenth century and those in the mid-1960s who were fighting for their children were middle-class. It was not that dyslexics were only found in that socio-economic group but because these parents had the means to seek help and were prepared to speak up. Hinshelwood's young boys were from middle-class families who were concerned that their children couldn't read and so took them to an ophthalmologist to see if they had faulty eyes; no NHS so this would have cost money. The children seen in the child guidance clinics would have been referred without the permission of their parents and were probably severely dyslexic and disruptive and as a result they stood out. Specialists of the era pointed out that by the time it was noticed that the child couldn't read he or she had been in school for a long time and remediation might not work. What was the point anyway as the child would have to have a manual job? Hinshelwood stood out against this practice but he was likely alone.

Similarly, in the 1960s, middle-class parents made the most noise. At the 1961 conference one parent who spoke up was a journalist and another was referred to as "a mother from Bath". So although it was difficult for parents of dyslexic children in the sixties to get help for their children, with the greater freedom of thought for all it was also more acceptable not to conform. Being middle-class was a double-edged sword for children from those families. The children benefited from their parents abilities and persistence but they carried a nudge, nudge stigma which must have been difficult to throw off.

Connections between charities and madness perhaps are more fanciful, but the social activities of the charities supporting the dyslexia movement would definitely have added to the myth of the "middle-class disease". Madness perhaps not, but cultural memories are long and deep. No-one wants to be different and parents are in the main protective of their offspring.

CHAPTER SIX

The Word Blind Centre

The "great conference" on the Word-blind in 1961[1] ended with as many questions as answers and the committee of the Invalid Children's Aid Association, having hosted it, proceeded with organizing the research and teaching programme. As the ICAA was a charity and not a university-based group, in order to undertake the project they first had to persuade a group of professionals to take part. Just as important, they also had to find a home, one in London, to house the researchers, the data and of course the children. This chapter paints a picture, gives a flavour of the place that resulted, and of those who worked there and the children that were helped. Much of the information it contains is taken from the minutes of the ICAA, its *Word Blind Children Bulletin*, reports from conferences and transcripts of interviews.

Many more people were involved in the centre than are written about here but those who appear are a good cross-section of the hard-working, pioneering individuals who took part (some of whom have already been introduced in *Chapter Four*). After the 1961 conference, Alfred White Franklin and Maisie Holt were anxious to start working on the issues raised. The phenomenon of word-blindness had created a host of unanswered questions such as what to do about diagnosis, which teaching methods to use and what research was needed, never mind the trickiest, "What is word-blindness?" To answer these a home had to be found where the teaching and research could happen and this became one of White Franklin's first tasks.

---

1. From 1963 re-named the *Word Blind Committee Bulletin*. Note again that although the first conference took place in 1961 the transcript was not published until 1962.

During his summing-up at the conference, Dr Gallagher had suggested that an association of like-minded people should be was formed and called something simple like "The Can't read, Can't spell" association. Immediately, a group was formed but was called the Association for Word Blind Children, and it comprised 70 registered members who were an eclectic mix of teachers, parents, speech therapists, doctors, education officers and educational psychologists, as well as MPs and industrialists. White Franklin put together a committee to head up the new association but also to be responsible for carrying out the proposals brought about by the conference. This committee was made up of some of the speakers at the conference together with eminent workers in the field.

On the first committee were: Dr Macdonald Critchley, Maisie Holt, Miss K Bird, Professor P Meredith, Dr T Miles, Professor O L Zangwill, Mr George Mitchell, Dr Kellmer Pringle and Sir Wilfred Sheldon. The chairman was Dr White Franklin and the secretaries Grace Rattenbury and Miss E Hilton. They were also secretaries to the ICAA, a point that would become important as the months passed. It is interesting to note that although the committee consisted of a wide range of individuals with influence who could help, including a "money man" in George Mitchell, there were no teachers, parents or dyslexics among the group other than Miss Bird, a co-principal of a school, and Maisie Holt who had taught children (but only as part of her clinical practice). The committee also had the problem of not having a dedicated university research base, although Meredith, Miles and Zangwill were all university researchers. They also had to cope with eccentrics like Patrick Meredith who was a mathematician and somewhat disorganized. Also with Maisie Holt as we will see.

The aims and objectives of the Word Blind Centre were later laid out clearly in *Specific Dyslexia* a report written by Sandhya Naidoo and published in 1972. In summary, the centre hoped to identify the nature and cause of specific dyslexia, to develop a battery of diagnostic tests, to examine and experiment with suitable teaching methods, to attempt to predict, through screening, young children who were likely to have specific dyslexia and to bring the findings to the notice of the general public as well as the Department of Education.

It was decided from the outset that the centre was to be a temporary research unit with a view to isolating the reasons for the disability referred to as "word-blindness" (which was also variously called specific dyslexia or just dyslexia). Teaching was to take place, but only as a means of researching the best methods of treating children with word-blindness. Last but not least was the teaching of the teachers, but this could only start after the other projects were off the ground and teaching methods were tried and tested. It was envisaged that the centre would run for five years and funding was sought for that length of time. However, not all parties involved accepted this position and this was to cause difficulties, so much so that decades later Tim Miles still emphasised the temporary nature when recounting the history of the centre.

Bart's saw the project start. Holt had been assessing and teaching word-blind children there for some ten years and as White Franklin was one of the hospital's senior paediatricians it was obvious thing to use the hospital and the word-blind children from Holt's existing and growing list. The movement had received interest from the press, both negative and positive, and as a result more and more parents of dyslexic children were trying to find help. Holt wrote of the events in her unpublished autobiography:[2]

> "The Conference was well pressed, and articles in various papers on the subject have appeared intermittently ever since. Also demands for lectures and discussion on the Radio and TV helped to spread information. Besides arousing much interest an unbelievable storm of abuse and opposition was also aroused, chiefly from teachers and Educational Psychologists who seemed to feel that their ability in their own particular field was being criticised or attacked. Such is the conservatism of the English.

> On the other hand the hospital now began to be besieged with enquiries and requests for treatment and lectures.

---

2. "Dyslexia—A Historical Account with Special Reference to England", date unknown. Courtesy of St Bartholomew's Hospital Archives.

As there was only one person to deal with all this, the waiting list was at one [or] two and a half years long. Many children were now referred directly to the Hospital by their doctor for suspected word blindness. They came from all over the country, as far afield as Lancashire, Wales, the North of England, Devon and Cornwall and even from foreign countries. They travelled to the Hospital once a week, for as long as was necessary, for one period of 45 minutes treatment. This was usually for 18 months to 2 years."[3]

Leaving the new centre at Bart's was not an option so White Franklin set to work trying to raise funds to enable the research to start and to find premises dedicated to the dual role of research and treatment.

The committee met regularly, almost on a monthly basis, in Macdonald Critchley's consulting rooms in Harley Street. According to Tim Miles the meetings were often tempestuous affairs but they did agree to produce a bulletin, charting the work of the centre. It was envisaged that it would be widely circulated, as was the paper from the 1961 conference. The bulletin was to be half newsletter half academic journal and would include articles from interested parties, the latest research papers, letters from parents and sections on children's work and teaching hints.

The committee soon hit stormy water and there were problems finding suitable accommodation. Members started to fall out, money was scarce and the whole venture was always under attack from the press and different educational, academic and research centres. The shock of how many enlisted men were illiterate during the Second World War had made politicians and educationalists alike realise that something had to be done to improve basic education. Free education had been available since 1870 but there were still many who could barely read a newspaper and the 1944 Education Act set out to improve the situation.

Rab Butler was fanatical about education and took the position of Minister of Education although he had been offered more senior positions in government. One of the tenets of the act was that all children had a right to education even if they were disabled. This of course applied

---

3.   Ibid.

to dyslexic children but as seen at the conference many educationalists were concerned about all non-readers rather than a small, specific group.

Many of the children being put forward as dyslexic were middle-class and came from homes where reading was the norm and as such were expected to read. For some, reading was not part of everyday life and though parents often did realise their children should read, and although they did their best to encourage and help, historically reading was not seen as a priority, and more importantly these children's vocabulary was often limited. So, and as seen in previous chapters, educationalists saw improving the lot of *all* children to be their number one aim and money being channelled to what could have been argued as an elite group went against the grain. This was not of course what the Word Blind Committee intended, rather they wanted to improve the lot of all children but did not want this particular group of sometimes bright children wasted.

White Franklin made it his business to search for money and a place for the centre to be located. He was a member of the executive committee of the Invalid Children's Aid Association (ICAA) and able to draw on the experience and contacts of the charity. As a stopgap, the centre started teaching at 4 Palace Gate, London, the ICAA HQ. The embryonic centre had one-and-a-half rooms in the bowels of the building and Helen Arkell, the first teacher, remembers working with children whilst seeing disembodied feet walking past the semi-basement windows. W P Payne, a visiting English teacher, wrote a description of the early days in an article for the bulletin:

"The Centre hides itself in a cluster of legations in Palace Gate Kensington. I waited in a gloomy hall on the first floor faced by a gigantic imitation Claude. There were partly made—and crudely made—bookcases by the picture, and occasionally doors opened to reveal office furniture that had never been to Heal's. Evidently the Word Blind Centre concentrated on essentials."[4]

---

4.   W P Payne, "Tas Whe Yo Wond, Ni Rifed!: A Visit to the Word Blind Centre", *Word Blind Committee Bulletin*, September 1965, Vol. 1, No. 4, p. 5.

Looking for more suitable accommodation was to take up a lot of the committee's time and patience and like all new ventures money was high on the list of priorities as without it nothing could begin. Although the centre had to be as low cost as possible, renting any space in central London came with a high price tag. The ICAA was offered a suit of rooms in Bartholomew Close but this is only mentioned once in the bulletin so must have fallen through. A venue in Shoreditch was suggested and turned down as not central enough, but possibly as it was not the trendy area it is today it was considered unsuitable for more reasons than one. The committee spent a lot of time discussing a house in Queen's Square. The plan was to use it prior to it being taken over by the National Children's Hospital; Macdonald Critchley had connections with this organization. This location was ideal and the committee was on the point of having the rooms decorated when the London County Council (LCC) turned down the planning application and White Franklin and the committee were thrown back into the search.

Running alongside the search for a home was the task of appointing staff. It was decided that the centre needed a director and advertisements were placed and notable members of the word-blind community were consulted, particularly Professor Gallagher and Ingrid Riis-Vestergaard who of course had both been speakers at the 1961 conference. Miles proposed Holt as deputy director with White Franklin as director, his plan being to make the director's post a titular position and use the deputy as the facilitator. On the surface this was a good idea but as time went by it became clear that this would not be the case. Holt's diagnostic and teaching methods were called into question, and she refused to give any clear reports or provide data on her "patients" as they were called. Possibly this was down to a clash of personalities making Holt defensive. For example, a report written about "DJP" to his doctor in 1963 lists clearly the tests used[5] when working with this eight-year-old boy; his reading and spelling ages, but no raw scores, the researchers would have wanted both. Holt did not include the raw scores but to do this would have been unlikely and unnecessary when communicating with

---

5.   These were Stamford Binet Revision, Burt Graded Word Scale, Midland Spelling tests, Schonnell S4, S5, S6 and S7, Bender Test and Ponteus Maze Test, all standard at the time.

the boy's doctor. It is not known whether she shared these findings with the Word Blind committee.

The arguments surrounding Maisie Holt went on for over a year and she raged about the lack of expertise of the teachers, who was on her client/patient list and who was on the centre's list. Holt felt that the ICAA had stepped in and taken over her domain. In some ways this was understandable as she had been working with children and adults, teaching and latterly assessing them, for more than ten years. Anecdotally her methods had been successful and she had helped a lot of people but she did not keep records. In conversation with Bevè Hornsby years later, she told me how she had worked with Holt and she had been "scary", not with the children but with her helpers, and was always "secretive".

Holt was on the original committee of the Association for Word Blind Children, but was infuriated when the committee became a sub-committee of the ICAA. Presumably she could see her influence waning in the shadow of a powerful charity. One can't help but feel sympathy for her, but the academics and researchers were desperate to give scientific credence to both the condition of word-blindness and the teaching methods and to do this they needed hard evidence.

In a letter to Grace Rattenbury in November 1963, Holt argues that there should be two sub-committees: one made up of educationalists to attend to the pressing need for treatment and training, and one to discuss research. She bemoans the loss of Professor Meredith, who had resigned from the committee, as she felt he should have chaired the research sub-committee. Professor Zangwill, in conversation with Rattenbury, comments that he thought Meredith resigned after only one year because he considered the committee were going in the wrong direction and that it (and presumably the embryonic centre) were not going to make "any important contribution to the problem". Miles refers to Meredith in his book *Dyslexia Research* as "rather eccentric" but also "highly imaginative and a creative thinker" so his going was a mixed blessing for the committee. Professor Meredith had some unusual methods of working with word-blind children loosely based on the Fernald method which no doubt would have been advantageous to the child in question but were time consuming and would have required the teacher to be thoroughly trained in his ideas. Also, Meredith was extremely anti IQ tests and these were becoming a major tool in the dyslexic assessment process. Holt's letter talks of her belief in word-blindness but she considers the centre would be unlikely to come up with proof of the condition when other, larger overseas establishments had not found cast-iron evidence. She presumably is referring to Orton and Monroe and their work in the USA and Scandinavian researchers. Holt does however take the credit for the funding provided for the centre though there is no written evidence of this. It is sad reading her letters to the committee as it is obvious that her main concerns were for the children and adults who had been referred to her. She thought that helping them through diagnosis and training should have been the centre's main priority. On the one hand she knew that establishing a method of diagnosis was important but she kept reiterating her rights to and ownership of "the waiting lists". It must have been heartbreaking but also irritating for White Franklin and other members of the committee trying to deal with her when their time would have been better spent setting up the centre and starting the research they knew was needed.

The search for a deputy director continued, Professor Gallagher and Ingrid Riis-Vestergaard recommended Dr Cole and Mrs Sally Child. The appointment of Sally Child continued to be discussed for some time. An American, she was trained in the Gillingham/Orton teaching methods and considered to be Anna Gillingham's successor. With an impressive CV she was prepared to work in London and/or teach instructors from the UK in the USA, but Child was expensive. In the early-1960s she was charging $100 a day, far more than the centre could afford, although she did suggest that she would charge less (details unavailable). The subject of Mrs Child went on being discussed by the committee for some years. Miles talked about her years later and of how the centre could not afford her fees.[6] Holt was greatly influenced by Child and ideally would have liked to have been deputy director under her but Child would have none of it, which indirectly contributed to Holt resigning.

---

6.   Interview with Tim Miles, 20th May 2004 at the University of North Wales, Bangor.

After a donation of £2,000 from Mrs Arnold Stuart, the committee was able to appointed Dr Alex Bannatyne (a New Zealander), an educational psychologist fresh from working in Australia. Bannatyne was not originally convinced by word-blindness but set about writing summaries and abstracts on all the literature on dyslexia he could find and toured the USA and Denmark looking at teaching methods, and soon the limited space at Palace Gate was stuffed full of paperwork. Once convinced of the syndrome Bannatyne like all converts became zealous in his research and work.

With an educational psychologist on board the centre now needed teaching staff. The committee immediately appointed Helen Arkell who was amazed at being summoned by the secretary to the ICAA, Kate Rackham and offered the job. Arkell was the most experienced teacher practising in the UK and, as a dyslexic herself, understood the condition. The hunt was on for other full-time teachers as Arkell was only able to work in London for a couple of days a week because she had other clients in Frensham, Surrey where she lived.

The committee drew up a list of possible teachers mainly trained in Scandinavia. Today finding teachers is an easy task but in 1963 this was an entirely different matter. Obviously there were teachers in the UK who had been successful in teaching dyslexics, but they were individuals working with their own methods and experience and were not necessarily using recognised schemes or teaching programmes. The teachers who were having success did not necessarily know they were dealing with word-blind children. However, the committee gathered together Helen Arkell and Mrs Hirsh and with Maisie Holt there was a teaching group, and with a place to teach Alfred White Franklin wrote in the winter bulletin of 1964, "And so we are off".

Helen Arkell had been teaching children from her home for some time and because of her experience of teaching dyslexics she had an article published in the second edition of the bulletin: "Reflections on Teaching the Word-blind". It is a lovely piece full of personal details, information on the problems of dyslexia but above all for parents hoping that their children would overcome their learning problems.

"In severe cases the sufferer will almost certainly remain illiterate unless he is given specialised teaching. Happily it is never too late for this and I have heard of a word-blind man of 55 learning to read and write."[7]

Perhaps as a result of family history, Arkell goes into detail about questioning parents as to whether there was a history of literacy problems in their own family. Heredity was a recurring theme for many researchers and teachers in the field but coming from Helen Arkell with her own family history it is particularly poignant. Arkell's credentials were perfect for all those concerned with the centre, even Holt approved of her; she was however the most self-effacing, diffident lady and appeared completely unaware of how important she was in those early days. It must have been Arkell that Payne writes of in his article about visiting the Word Blind Centre. He was shown around and watched a "Danish trained teacher" working with a boy saying, "I felt how fortunate the boy was to have an adult devote her intelligent sympathy and her understanding to him in his difficulties."[8]

Arkell worked part-time at the centre and the full-time teacher was Mrs Hirsch, who had previously been a remedial teacher probably with one of the child guidance clinics. Unfortunately Mrs Hirsch became ill and after a short time she died was replaced by Gill Cotterell. In October 1964 there were more requests for testing and the first indicator of Mrs Hirsch's illness, she was absent with a toothache. Mrs Hirsch did get to visit the Word Blind Institute in Copenhagen with Alex Bannatyne before she became too ill. Her only contribution to the bulletin was a teaching aid "ea" phonemes:

The Meagre Eater Teacher

I heard of a teacher last year
Who could balance herself on each ear.
"I shall not repeat

7.   Helen Arkell, "Reflections on Teaching the Word-blind", *Word Blind Committee Bulletin*, October 1963, pp. 4–5.
8.   W P Payne, "Tas Whe Yo Wond, Ni Rifed! A Visit to the Word Blind Centre", *Word Blind Committee Bulletin*, September 1965, Vol. 1, No. 4, pp. 5–7.

Such a heavenly feat!"
She breathed in a voice soft and clear.
So she zealously stood on her head,
Eating meals of cheap crusty bread
Until, hungry and weak,
She fell down with a squeak
And had a good breakfast instead.[9]

Numerous teachers' names appear in the literature: Miss B Warburton (who later became Mrs Allan), Mrs McCowan, Mrs Woodman, E M Bradshaw, but Gill Cotterell and Helen Arkell are particularly remembered as they went on to work in and write about dyslexia. All the teachers at the centre made it a magical place for children who had been little understood until this moment in time in the midst of the "swinging sixties".

The bulletin was the voice of the Word Blind Centre and in the first publication in February 1963 the committee laid out their case for dyslexia. The current thinking on education in the early-1960s was almost completely at odds with them. Professor P Meredith wrote in the first edition that there was "an ill-defined theoretical concept of a 'spectrum' or 'continuum' of reading disability". He argued that dyslexics had a particular set of problems that could be overcome, and that they were not just a sub-group of non-readers. The popular argument was that there was a "continuum" of non-readers who would, with time, achieve some level of reading ability through the normal teaching methods used in schools. A group of educational psychologists, including Dr Daniels who spoke at the conference, argued that, if they agreed that dyslexia existed, by necessity that would mean that dyslexics were untreatable because they were brain damaged. Although those working in the field thought it was possible that only severely dyslexic children were mildly brain damaged they knew even they could be taught given the appropriate teaching methods because it had been done.

---

9.   Esther Hirsch, "The Meagre Eater Teacher", *Word Blind Committee Bulletin,* Winter 1966, Vol. 1, Nos. 6 and 7, p. 21.

Another battle being faced by the pioneers was post-Freudian and post-Kleinian thinking, the popular philosophy of the day, that all children's problems other than physical disabilities were the fault of their home life rather than any neurological differences. As discussed in a previous chapter the timing of the Word Blind Centre was right in the middle of the movement for child-centred education. The centre was not at odds with the best of this teaching but realised that informal teaching methods did not help children who needed structure to learn. Professor Meredith finished his article claiming that the Word Blind Committee

"is a hard-working committee, determined to press on with all possible speed towards the provision of facilities for opening the world of the written word to those for whom normal education has failed to open the door."[10]

In the second bulletin in October 1963, Macdonald Critchley is once again making a case for dyslexics being a separate group to other non-readers and a group he had frequently come across.[11] Critchley is witty in his list of excuses for non-reading dyslexics given by sceptical educationalist: neurosis, mental retardation, teaching methods, teaching a child at too young an age, or too old an age, birth trauma or even too many children in a family. He concludes:

"Such muddled thinking would be amusing if the problem was not so serious, and in that these notions of multiple aetiology have led to the regrettable result that there has been no consistent policy to help the majority of the unfortunate victims."[12]

Of course most children, even with home and health problems, learn to read and these otherwise bright children struggling to do what others did almost by magic was what was confounding those working in the

---

10. G Patrick Meredith, "The Association for Word Blind Children", *The Association for Word Blind Children Bulletin*, February 1963, p. 2.
11. The article originally was written for the Proceedings of the Royal Society of Medicine and reproduced in the 1963 bulletin.
12. Macdonald Critchley, "The Problem of Developmental Dyslexia", *Word Blind Committee Bulletin*, October 1963, p. 2.

field. Later in his article, Critchley warns against seeing the condition as a mirror of the results seen in brain damaged adults. Although some of the symptoms were similar he was convinced that if an autopsy was undertaken on the brain of a developmental dyslexic lesions would not be found. He obviously longed to see into the brain of the children he was working with but it would be a long time before this was possible.

Tim Miles' contribution to the first bulletin was what seemed like a "diatribe" against an article in an HMSO publication, *The Health of the School Child 1962: Dyslexia*. It must have been published at roughly the same time as the conference and in Miles' estimation was written by a medical officer with little or no experience of dyslexia. He disapproved of the sample of children tested, the testing methods, the length of time taken over the tests and the outcome. Miles was well-known for his attention to detail and he appears to consider this piece of work not only to be shoddy but also detrimental to the dyslexic cause.

As a counter balance to his first article, in the second bulletin Miles presents *A Dialogue On Definition* where he has an imaginary conversation answering many of the questions being asked in the press and elsewhere as to what was dyslexia. He cleverly laid out the conditions that are present in all dyslexic children followed by the other symptoms that might occur. He took all the criticisms and questions from educationalists, educational psychologists, and the media and answered them squarely. Tim Miles and his wife Elaine went on to develop a diagnostic tool for identifying dyslexia, the Bangor Dyslexia Test, and the germ for that idea could well have been this article.

Maisie Holt's article in the first edition of the bulletin is also an attempt to explain dyslexia and may have been included as an advertisement to encourage parents to bring their children for help. Holt described the effect dyslexia had on children, symptoms to look out for and how correct remediation was necessary to correct or improve the condition. Two boys were cited in the article both of whom had improved with help.

At this stage the need for a proper home was always high on the committee's agenda. The rooms in Palace Gate were only a temporary measure and other venues had not panned out but at last, through ICAA contacts, the committee were offered a small building in Coram's Fields (which had been a lavatory block).

Today Coram's Fields is still an amazing place, a green oasis in the centre of London dedicated to children, and everyone who knows of it quotes the sign above the entrance that adults are only permitted to enter if accompanied by a child under 16. Thomas Coram, a shipwright, in 1722 walked the streets of London as part of his job, particularly a route between his shipyard in Rotherhithe and business premises in the City of London which led him see abandoned babies left to die in the gutter. He was a down to earth man, married but childless and a devout Anglican and was horrified by this practice. He set about raising the funds to start a foundling hospital. Such institutions, though common in Europe, were not previously seen in England. Babies born out of wedlock were not only unwanted but their mothers were seen as morally degenerate, fathers were never blamed.

Coram was successful in his campaign to save some of the babies though it took him 17 years to raise the money. He persuaded numerous well-known people, Horace Walpole, Hogarth, dukes, duchesses and royal patrons to take an interest. Sadly Coram's plain speaking and common sense did not stand him in good stead and when the hospital was opened he fell out with the committee and was ousted by his noble patrons and only saw his foundling children in the role of godfather. The site has continued to bear Coram's name. In 1964 the main buildings were being demolished to build a new assessment and rehabilitation centre for the Institute of Child Health and by a miracle one of Alfred White Franklin's contacts managed to stop the demolition of the lavatory wing. With what remained of the buildings it was possible to make teaching rooms and offices and later terrapin teaching rooms were added, known by Tim Miles and his friends as "The Caravans".

Mr Gordon Piller the house governor of the Great Ormond Street Hospital for Children, had secured this small building from the LCC and funding was sought and found from two charities the Children's Research Fund and the City Parochial Foundation. White Franklin in applying for funding to Lord Cohen of Birkenhead writes a detailed letter with estimated costs but one is in wonder at the simplicity of the process, which yielded £15,000, a not inconsiderable sum in the 1960s. The buildings which were then owned by the Institute of Child Health were loaned to the ICAA for the Word Blind Centre rent free for the duration of their project, or until the institute required them for rebuilding. The ICAA in return was responsible for the upkeep, utilities, etc.

On the 30th September 1964, Alex Bannatyne and Alfred White Franklin with Elizabeth Kirkwood, the centre's administrator in attendance, were shown around the building at Coram's Fields. From the outset it was seen that the space was not adequate for their needs but with the addition of an extra building it would suffice. The repairs and decorating were to be paid for out of the grant from the Children's Research Fund and in notes of the meeting copied to Bannatyne and White Franklin there are lovely little details such as "who will mend the holes in the path" and next to requirements for the general office a hand written note asks for "3 hooks" as opposed to a "coat rack to be put up", suggesting limited funds.

The centre was to have an entrance hall off which was a general office and a cloakroom. Alex Bannatyne had a room to himself and the assistant psychologist was to use the room which doubled as a medical room. There were two teaching rooms in the main building and a second cloakroom for children and parents. Two more rooms were later constructed in the temporary terrapin, but at the time of Bannatyne and White Franklin's visit the idea was to build an annex attached to the main building. Surrounding the centre a wattle fence was erected to screen it from the hospital building site and it was decided to join the classrooms with an external covered walkway. Mention in the minutes is made of windows and skylights indicating how important the doctors considered the children's surroundings to be, making them as light, airy and comfortable as possible. Grace Rattenbury and Elizabeth Kirkwood were responsible for the details of the plans and organized the programme of work, and at last the Word Blind Centre had a home.

In the final edition of the bulletin Sandhya Naidoo reminisces about the Word Blind Centre and her first sight of the building. In 1966 when she arrived, she had been expecting a sizeable building as the centre was by this time famous. Not only did it appear frequently in the media but had been officially opened by Princess Margaret, but what she found was "a little cottage". The small entrance hall was always full of comings and goings. Parents had to wait, often for a considerable amount of time while their children were diagnosed or taught. This time was usefully spent exchanging information and often gaining comfort from finding that they were not the only parents with dyslexic children. Others waiting were visiting educationalists from home and abroad and Sandhya Naidoo wrote of her amusement at the faces of these visitors as they mirrored her original amazement at the size of this bustling little place.

Wednesday was the busiest and most congested day at the centre as this was when White Franklin examined children who had been recommended to it. It was also the day when all the members of staff squashed together to eat a packed lunch and take part in an impromptu staff meeting. There were nine staff working there at any one time and this Naidoo said made an ideal number to sit around a table. The cooperation and informal interaction between all staff members allowed for a full and complete profile to be made of each child in their care. Today this practice would be commonplace but in the 1960s attitudes were normally more formal. Even at the centre, Cotterell, in interview, explained that as a teacher she did not have a lot to do with White Franklin, who was a typical consultant, and it sounds as though the place was somewhat hierarchical. In the early days he did some of the assessments but more were undertaken by Macdonald Critchley and David Mosely. Later, other educational psychologists were added to the list including Tim Miles.

The secretaries were the first point of contact at both the centre and the ICAA and were sympathetic as well as being a mine of information. Parents would phone confused and frustrated and unload all their worries before the secretary could pinpoint their particular needs and advise on the best cause of action. In *Specific Dyslexia*, Naidoo explains that each child who arrived at the centre was given advice but that not all the children who presented were suitable for the research: some had severe emotional problems, others were physically disabled and yet others had some literacy problems but were just not bad enough for the study. All comers however were considered and given recommendations of the best way forward for them.

Many children lived too far from the centre and attendance would have been impractical. Children were seen from all over England and Wales, as far afield as Yorkshire, Northumberland and Cardiganshire (Ceredigion) as well as from overseas (as noted in the handwritten register with addresses in Kenya, Uganda, Malta, Switzerland, Germany, Ceylon (Sri Lanka) and the USA). Some of these children were stationed in London but it must be presumed that some were there specifically to be assessed.

Most of the overseas children were referred by their parents. In the register there is no distinction made between children who were unsuitable or those who just lived too far away to make weekly visits to it viable, but the centre records show that all those who live outside of London and the Home Counties were turned down. The bulletin refers to this problem and makes the point that in all cases the centre staff made contact with a child's school or child guidance clinic with advice.

In 1963, the fledgling centre had 100 children diagnosed as word-blind. It had the backing of the Department of Education and Science but of course it was the teaching that the department was interested in rather than the research. The centre tried to encourage children's schools with advice as to how to undertake teaching. A letter to Bannatyne from a headteacher survives stating that the school was aware of the child's problems but staff shortages had left him without help. Another concerning a child assessed and selected for research by White Franklin has the education office asking the boy's school to release him from school to attend sessions at the centre and the department agreeing to pay a fee of three guineas for a teaching session.[13]

Alex Bannatyne did not stay long. He toured the dyslexia centres of Scandinavia and the USA and collected a phenomenal amount of data on the subject of word-blindness. With a view to starting the research project, he began looking for "pairs". He became fanatical about pairing groups of dyslexic children with non-dyslexic children to act as "norms". He fell out with Holt in a big way because she did not keep clear records of the children she saw at Bart's, so those she worked with were not suitable for the studies. It wasn't just Bannatyne. The Local Education

---

13. A guinea was £1 1 shilling (£1.05. Around £21 today allowing for inflation).

Authorities (LEAs) were concerned that Holt's history of record-keeping was too erratic and as the centre needed the LEAs for funding it became necessary for Holt not to be involved. It appears she would say she had evidence of this and that, quoting numbers at random. Miles said the numbers changed from day-to-day and there was no solid evidence. This rattled the committee as its members were all trying to prove the condition with research which by the nature of dyslexia was difficult enough, so people like Holt must have been an anathema.

Bannatyne writes to White Franklin begging that Holt be asked to resign from the Word Blind project; at one point in this letter he asks if she is even a qualified teacher. He is so angry that he writes that he knows Holt would have to be allowed to continue with the group of children she is already seeing but that these children would be useless to the centre's research because of her methods. Miles used to stay with Holt on the occasions that he came to London from Bangor for committee meetings. When White Franklin was dealing with the row between Holt and Bannatyne he was scared Miles might jump ship and he contacted Miles but the centre was too important to Miles to give it up for Holt. Holt probably used a phonic method based on the Gillingham/Stillman model as she knew Sally Child. The dyslexia movement has continued with this rather secretive approach to teaching dyslexics and perhaps it started with Holt.

Bannatyne's insistence on the correct procedures was right and proper, being the only way to carry out scientific research. Where he fell down was in trying to prove the existence of sub-groups, which became more and more detailed and specific. Each dyslexic type he looked into also needed a "norm", same gender, same intelligence and same group, but the centre was just not in touch with a wide enough range of children to do this. In the winter edition of the bulletin, Bannatyne describes what he considered to be the sub-sections of dyslexia and lists his aims for two research projects, one looking at the causes of dyslexia and one treatment. As an example of his detailed approach to research is the title of the first project in his words: "A Psycho-Neurological Research in the Aetiology of Specific Developmental Dyslexia in Children". The aims for this project were as intricate as the title and are listed verbatim as a footnote.[14] The title of the second research project was: "The Evaluation of Remedial Techniques for Use with Dyslexic Children."

Bannatyne had looked at teaching methods from the USA, Scandinavia and the UK in his search for the perfect learning scheme. However, he surmises that even before the project started he suspected it would be necessary to select, from amongst the differing methods, programmes to suit each individual child:

> "It is not unlikely that most of the techniques may prove to be of benefit to different kinds of dyslexic children (if different kinds exist) and that the research will assist in the matching of method to child."[15]

Bannatyne's intention was to gather a group of 60 children covering three age groups. To eliminate any social bias he hoped to test many children, presumably in London, and use every "n'th" child. He knew that the children presenting at Bart's and the centre were likely to come from mainly one socio-economic group and this he saw as dangerous. He also required a norm group mirroring the dyslexic group as far as age, intelligence, etc. but who had no literacy problems. To gather the dyslexic children, Bannatyne intended to call on the services of the different institutions involved with word-blind children and at the end of the article he says that he has the agreement of "various hospitals and colleges" to help undertake the research. By subjecting the two groups of children to a formidable battery of tests Bannatyne hoped to arrive at a set of differences seen only in the dyslexic child and that these oddities could then be investigated giving clues to the cause of dyslexia. With the results Bannatyne proposed working with a computer specialist to

---

14. "1. To explore the incidence of the various symptoms of dyslexia in a selected sample of children. 2. To discover the correlational links of these symptoms with physiological, neurological, and psychological attributes. 3. To discriminate statistically (in terms of these key attributes) between dyslexic children and children who can read and spell well. 4. To trace back to the primary causes of dyslexia by using the information gained from the above exploratory stages. 5. To establish experimentally if dyslexia is a single 'amorphous' disability among dyslexics or if several types separately exist, at least in terms of several original causes. 6. To discover if dyslexia (or each type of dyslexia separately) is a population continuum in its distribution or whether it is a scattered phenomenon of isolated disability".

15. Alex Bannatyne, "Research Needs in Dyslexia", *Word Blind Committee Bulletin*, Winter 1964/65, Vol. 1, No. 4, pp. 5–6.

form patterns. This technique had been used before with other disabilities. He quoted aphasia. These patterns would provide pointers for the researchers to work on.

The teaching methods being used would pose problems not because the methods had any inherent failings but in that the method relied heavily on the expertise of the teacher and Bannatyne's awareness that any new technique kept a child's attention for a while. Bannatyne was also aware that the teachers tended to favour the methods they considered most practical and effective. To acquire a satisfactory set of results it was necessary to have a large group of children and a lot of data, which he hoped would be gathered over the years by the centre. However the amount of material required would have been phenomenal and time was running out, there were only three years left for the Word Blind Centre.

By the 1966 winter edition of the *Word Blind Committee Bulletin,* Dr Bannatyne was seen leaving the centre to follow a career in "The Psychology of Language" at the University of Illinois, USA and White Franklin is urging the reader to view Dr Bannatyne's classifications of dyslexia as his own and not necessarily the opinion of the committee.

Alex Bannatyne left a lasting legacy as can be seen subsequently from his many articles and books. Teachers like Gill Cotterell who worked with him in London found him to be charismatic and inspirational. His final article for the bulletin is complex and rambling but the conclusions, unlike the earlier sections in the paper, are clear. Dyslexics should always be seen as individuals, each with a separate list of needs and therefore each requiring an individual programme of therapy.

"The temptation must be resisted to find and to use 'one method, one panacea' for all types of children in this as in education in general." [16]

Miles' comments were:

---

16. Alex Bannatyne, "Diagnostic and Remedial Techniques for Use with Dyslexic Children", *Word Blind Committee Bulletin,* Winter 1966, Vol. 1. Nos. 6 and 7, p. 12.

"He didn't stay long, but subsequently made many valuable contributions to dyslexia work in the USA."[17]

Bannatyne's thoughts and conclusions were probably based on observation. He considered that there were three types of dyslexia: Primary Emotional Communicative Dyslexia, Minimal Neurological Dysfunction Dyslexia and Genetic Dyslexia. The first occurs because of poor parenting, the second is mild brain damage and the third is an inherited syndrome. The reasoning behind each type was argued over using other researchers' work. As Bannatyne's conclusions were not based on the work of the centre this was presumably why White Franklin distanced himself from the article in the Foreword to this edition of the bulletin.

"Nor is the content of the articles guaranteed in any way either by the editor or, still less, by members of the Word Blind Committee. This applies particularly to this number. Dr Alex Bannatyne has suggested a classification of the dyslexia and writes further about diagnosis and treatment. Neither he nor anyone else concerned with the Centre makes the assumption that the classification is now established beyond doubt and on a case record. This is still a tentative suggestion put forward as a basis for further discussion and for testing by actual case experience."[18]

Arthur White Franklin resigned as chairman of the ICAA in November 1964 due to pressure of work. He was the tenth chairman and had held the post for nine years. On retirement he was presented with a gift from those working in the ICAA by Princess Margaret at an annual general meeting of the society, a crystal decanter and glasses. He resigned from the ICAA but of course not from the centre where he continued as honorary medical officer until the end.

By 1966 children were arriving from all over London as well as much further afield; they were assessed by one of a group of educational psychologists under the guidance of White Franklin and Macdonald Critchley.

---

17. Interview One, 2002.
18. Alfred White Franklin, "Foreword", Winter 1966, Vol. 1., Nos. 6 and 7, p. 2.

ossible they were given tuition at the centre, and if this wasn't possible advice was given to schools and child guidance clinics.

There was so much interest raised by the centre that it was necessary to get the teaching courses started. Of course dyslexics had been taught prior to 1961, but the teaching methods had not been gathered together and given a name. The techniques needed to be intricate and structured but the basic concept was always multi-sensory input. In other words the teacher would teach using all of a child's senses, visual, auditory, kinaesthetic (seeing, hearing and feeling), plus the other less obvious senses such as a sense of humour, any means to cement a concept into the child's long term memory. As seen, many of the teacher's using these techniques in the 1960s came from the USA and Denmark. At the centre each child was taught as an individual or in a small group in about 40–60 minute sessions; the time was split into small chunks of around ten minutes. Emphasis was placed on the lesson being fun; trying to avoid the child failing; and games were often used to reinforce a particular element being taught.

Although there are reports and opinions of the centre written by professionals and journalists it is more difficult to gauge how the children felt. The maximum length of time that any one child spent at the centre was two years and for some it was less. They attended once a week during term time and there appears to have been a maximum of 45 children at any one time. One insight into the feelings of the children was through the television programme *24 Hours* in which the BBC did a ten minute slot about the centre, and the excitement caused by the film crew and Michael Parkinson,[19] the presenter, was remembered long after by the teachers and psychologists. Parkinson introduced the item with some shocking statistics as to the number of children leaving primary schools with low levels of literacy: 8,000 children nationally at the age of seven not reading and another 25 per cent struggling. He explained that some parents were not prepared to leave the responsibility for teaching their children to read to the schools.

---

19.   Michael Parkinson was at the beginning of his career as a TV presenter and although already well-known was nowhere near as famous as he later became.

A Mr MacDuff, the father of George, had withdrawn his son from school because he was placed in the D stream as, although he was otherwise intelligent, he was not reading. He set about improving his son's literacy skills and by the time he was eleven an educational psychologist considered he was capable of passing the eleven plus, the goal of many parents at the time. George did not obtain a grammar school place and his father felt that if his difficulties had been noticed by teachers earlier this would not have been the case. MacDuff said bitterly that D level stood for "discard".

At this point, and no doubt to the excitement of those involved, the cameras moved to the Word Blind Centre. Two children were interviewed, an eleven-year-old girl called Tanya and 13-year-old boy called David. Tanya was shy and reticent but she managed to tell Parkinson how she had struggled in infant and junior schools. David was more articulate as he recounted his history of distress at his old school, which had resulted in two weeks in hospital; after that he had been referred to the centre by his doctor. By the time of the programme David was feeling positive, his literacy skills had improved and he was "more comfortable" in himself.[20] Tanya must have been so upset when Parkinson asked her to spell two words aloud, "strength" and "except". She failed but more importantly the brave little girl was able to explain how it felt to not be able to identify the sound-image bond that is necessary to spelling. Tanya had sat at the bottom of her primary classes with baby books, which she admitted she had memorised (echoes of children being tested by inspectors in days gone by). Tanya's reading improved during her time at the centre but her spelling age still lagged behind her reading age.

Gill Cotterell now took centre stage and in a few minutes explained the main problems a child has with dyslexia and she called for early identification (by seven to eight years) to give a child the maximum benefit of therapeutic teaching. Cotterell said that early diagnosis was rare in mainstream schools as at the time the class sizes were huge, non-readers were just considered to be "dull". There were few if any facilities in schools for special teaching and, countrywide, there were few educational

---

20. Words transcribed from the programme.

psychologists to diagnose problems. In Cotterell's opinion the most intelligent dyslexics learnt to read without remedial teaching, but spelling remained a problem for them, continuing into adulthood.

I contacted and interviewed one adult who had been a child at the centre. A was 14 when he was given a place there in October 1964. His mother was aware of dyslexia because his brother was mildly dyslexic. He was recommended to see Dr Bannantyne by an educational psychologist in Tunbridge Wells and was interviewed at Queen's Gate prior to the opening of the centre. He was accepted by Bannantyne and taught by Gill Cotterell at Coram's Fields. A's most vivid memory of his time at the centre were not the teaching methods but his journeys to and from Sussex where he was at school. As a 14-year-old he was most interested in missing games and saving some of his travel money to buy baked beans. A was used in the research programme and the phonetic reading cards made by him still exist. A remembers with pleasure the relaxed atmosphere of Coram's Fields away from the tensions of school. He went on to become one of Tim Miles first dyslexic undergraduates at Bangor and took part in the 1970 conference on dyslexia.

In Tim Miles' papers at Bangor are some tantalising glimpses of the workings of the centre and of the children. For example, notes about a boy M W who was taught by the centre during the transition from Bart's to Coram's Fields. He was first seen by Mrs Hirsch and White Franklin on the 7th June 1963 after his parents had read an article in the *Sunday Times* (17th March 1963). On 25 April 1963, M W's father sent the centre a letter referring to reports and assessments by psychologists. Rattenbury and White Franklin communicated formally over the paperwork that was necessary and by August 1964 MW was offered a place for an hour twice weekly. The family were expected to contribute by filling in questionnaires and going to interviews with the staff, Bannantyne and Mrs Hirsch being two of the interviewers. On the 4th September 1964 M W's headteacher was sent a progress report. M W was seen at Bart's so he got caught up with the arguments with Holt as to who were her clients and who were the centre's, but White Franklin won out with MW and he was offered a place at Coram's Fields. However M W did not get to go to Coram's Fields as in August his family moved to Manchester.

Parents were not always easy to deal with as the following example reveals. On the 22nd September 1967 an American child was presented to Sandhya Naidoo for assessment, Naidoo felt he needed tuition and was suitable for the centre but was only going to be in the UK for one year. The centre managed to fit him in, but it was decided that his fees should not be paid by the Inner London Education Authority (ILEA) and his parents were happy to pay. Kate Rackham appears in the letters as the ICAA secretary for schools; she was weighed down with requests and didn't always manage to get the paperwork together. The parents emerge as pushy and they inundated the child's future school and the centre with requests, however it agreed to teach him. His first report was written by Cotterell and shows progress, it was countersigned by Naidoo.

In October 1967 Naidoo writes to the child's school explaining the situation re his educational standing and when they can start teaching him and recommends the school adopt a phonic approach to teaching the boy. In line with the research programme in November 1967, White Franklin writes to the mother's hospital in New York asking for details of her birth and post-natal situation as the child has some motor-skill weakness. After all this work the parents decide to take the child on holiday before the end of term in May 1968 and Naidoo gets tough and says he has to leave at the beginning of the summer term as she has a waiting list.

Fights with LEAs were not uncommon. In 1968, the centre agreed to see a child with reasonable reading skills but poor spelling. They discovered that he had an IQ of 130 and decided to offer him help during the school summer vacation[21] in the hope that this would make a difference to him and give his school something to work on. It was agreed that he would have ten sessions through the summer with Cotterell at two guineas a time. As he had also seen White Franklin, he does his usual thing of writing to the mother's obstetrician. At the end of the summer Naidoo thinks he still needs help and writes to his LEA asking if they have any facilities. In the meantime, White Franklin writes a report showing strong familial findings and suggests the boy is given a full assessment and proposes that he is included on the research programme. Naidoo

---

21. The centre appears to have kept going through the summer, in fact through all the holidays. Later there is a note of a child seen on the 23rd December.

receives no help for the boy from his LEA as they consider his literacy problems are not severe enough. Naidoo puts him on the centre's waiting list but cannot promise a place. A single place comes up in November 1968 and is offered to the child, plus extra help during the Easter break. He does improve but leaves at the end of prep school. The letters and reports imply this was an unhappy little boy.

Another child, a girl this time in 1970, caused letters to fly between the centre and one LEA. She was recommended by Macdonald Critchley; she could read reasonably well but had weak spelling skills. All agreed that she should have a place but that she had to go on the waiting list. The centre asked her LEA for fees, which by June 1970 were £57.15.0d for two sessions per week for a term, and on the 7th August 1970 she was offered a place for September. However her school was not prepared to let her out of lessons in the mornings and the LEA took the opportunity not to pay up straightaway, wanting to see evidence of discussion between the centre and the school. The LEA at this point decided that the girl did not have severe problems and that she could be supported by their area centre. Reports of a telephone conversation indicate informally and off the record that the authorities did not approve of parents using private consultants like Critchley or of sending their children to private school and then expecting financial help in sending them to the centre. It was decided that the child probably only required two terms support, especially as her school was being helpful.

The parents indicated that they were cross with the authority as they had intended to make a donation to the centre but would now not be able to. Have attitudes today changed as to the ethics of parents? In March 1971 the parents of the girl were further thrown by a letter from the centre explaining that it was to close in August. The girl's mother panicked as to where her daughter was to go for help as although she had a place at Millfield that would not be until she was 13. The mother suggested a Swiss school but everyone disagreed with this idea. The teachers at the centre suggested she go to the local comprehensive; was this suggestion ironic?

The Word Blind Centre took a long-term interest in the children that came through its doors. In the Bangor papers are notes of a boy who was referred on the 23rd December 1965. It is a straightforward record but interesting again because of the funding. Harrow LEA was paying his fees and at one point towards the end of his time attending there was a mix up and it appeared that this had been withdrawn. The parents paid but the authority found out and the matter was resolved. The centre stayed in touch with the family offering help where it could, at one point in 1970 suggesting a unit in Camberwell that worked with adults that might help him. The record indicates that he had progressed well as he asked for a certificate for "extra time provision" to help him in taking his BSc examinations in electronics.

In 1978 Cambridge University's education department looked at a group of adults who as children had been clients of the centre. The ICAA allowed it access to the case histories of these children and the original interviewers included Mrs Wattle who had been on the fringes of the centre at the time of the original research. Miles was party to the research in that he encouraged Wattle to undertake the work. Included in the study are comments made by the adults and these give an insight into their feelings and fears as children. Pre-entry to the centre the comments about their schooling were negative: "dreaded junior school", "hated school—avoided it as much as possible", "school refused help with remediation"—whereas after they had attended the centre their schools began to take more notice of them and provided help and perhaps the most positive result; the schools stopped considering them to be "abnormal".

The heartfelt comments on the emotional support that had been received by the children were terrific: "Word Blind Centre a 'life-saver'", "Word Blind Centre great improvement", "Even spelling acceptable", "Word Blind Centre helped (me) to understand problems. Remediation made 'O' level passes possible". The report from the 1978 research *Coping With Dyslexia* was written up by David Bruce and he describes tellingly the general feeling of those interviewed:

"However, something else was gained through attendance at the Centre in addition to any possible improvement in skills. The diagnosis of dyslexia generally brought a feeling of relief and determination to achieve despite the handicap. This determination was still very evident in the interview schedules, though often tinged with wistfulness as ambitions moved further out of reach."[22]

Robert Somervell was aware of the work undertaken by the Cambridge group and felt that their findings were unnecessarily pessimistic. He attempted to contact 57 Word Blind Centre students in the late-1970s and early-1980s. He writes cheerfully of leaving Tim Miles' office with two carrier bags stuffed full of personal files. He sent each student a questionnaire asking for information on their present occupation and their attitude to being dyslexic and being known as dyslexic. In Miles' papers is a list of 13 people who replied giving their qualifications and present occupation; of these one had a first degree and four had first and second degrees. The remaining eight had all achieved qualifications and were in employment, one having founded a micro-electronics company and in brackets it stated "Owns a Ferrari".

Somervell followed up one of the cases, a success story. DJP was tested by Holt and attended the centre and had further classes with Helen Arkell and her daughter. He had a chequered school life but eventually found his footing and went to Churchill College Cambridge where he studied English. From Cambridge he went on to the Royal College of Arts where he gained a PhD in Holography. Although like most young dyslexics his life was chaotic, he looked back on the centre with affection.[23]

In the 1966 edition of the bulletin, White Franklin welcomed Sandhya Naidoo to the centre. Her first job was to revamp the proposals made by Bannantyne. The money raised was for research but somehow it had to fund the assessment, teaching and research. Naidoo suggested that assessments be undertaken free of charge but a fee was made for the teaching. In the main the fees were paid by LEAs; a few parents paid but not many.

In interview, Naidoo remembered clearly those early days. It was essential to lay down the criteria necessary to form a research group using the

---

22. David Bruce, "Coping With Dyslexia", *Cambridge Journal of Education,* November 1983, Vol. 13, Issue 3, p. 16.
23. Somervell in a letter to Arkell about DJP comments that one of her lectures left him with an abiding interest in dyslexia and he went on to work in his local dyslexia association as well as the British Dyslexia Association for the rest of his life. He died in 2010.

children they had already assessed. Naidoo devised a battery of tests which looked at the aetiology (causes): family connections, left-handedness, associated symptoms, auditory and visual problems, language, speech, father's occupation, socio-economic group, it was a huge list of criteria. The centre was active in making suggestions or agreeing with her ideas; Naidoo said they were helpful. She started in September and had the proposal finished by the end of the year; as she had been working in the area she modestly said it hadn't been that difficult. As to the strong attitude against IQ tests at the time, Naidoo understood why, but by using something like the Wechsler Intelligence Scale for Children (WISC)[24] they could use the profile ("there were some wonderful profiles", "profiles are very telling").[25] Part of the criteria was for the child to have a verbal IQ of at least 90. As they were looking at a reading problem the team were not so worried about the non-verbal IQ. Naidoo, however, saw word-blindness as a "whole life problem" not just a lack of reading and spelling abilities.

The research funding wasn't forever, originally only for five years, so it was important for the team to get a move on. Naidoo had a research assistant to look at all of the data they were coming up with, and as they wanted to exclude any child they considered wasn't dyslexic they had the schools use the Bristol Social Assessment Guide to rule out children with personality problems. The assistant looked at all the children assessed and pulled out those that met the criteria. These children were mainly middle-class, simply because they were the children who had been brought forward, so it was especially important because of the usual jibes to scrupulously match these children with "norms". The centre used one state school and two private schools and the children were randomly selected and matched on age. This assessment threw up 98 children in all, 55 referred to as the reading retard group and 42 as spelling retards and these were matched with control groups so there were four groups

---

24. A series of tests the results of which added together give the IQ of the child. Stanford Binet (often discussed in the same context) is similar. The dyslexic world used the WISC because most people when tested have a similar reading for each test, but dyslexics have a varied profile, they are good at some things and bad at others. Their "spikey" profile is said to denote dyslexia.
25. Words in quotes from my interview of 10th August 2004.

in all. The researchers didn't test the controls to see if any had reading or spelling problems. That was left open.

It turned out to be a complex study and as Bannatyne had thought required computers to analyse the data; normal today but revolutionary in the 1960s. Someone suggested asking Harvey Goldstein a lecturer in statistics at the Institute of Child Health, which was just across the road, to help. Naidoo said they couldn't have completed the project without Harvey and he worked out how they could analyse and compare the four groups. By this time the team realised there wasn't a single group and wanted to know if that point could be taken into consideration. Harvey said yes and to do this he got in touch with Rothemstow Agricultural programme and used cluster analysis. The image produced was eventually used on the dust-cover of Naidoo's book *Specific Dyslexia*.

There were two bulletins in 1967 and the first mainly concentrated on "reading". The Forewords give a flavour of how frustrated the team were that the whole subject of dyslexia was not being taken more seriously and was being played down by other experts in the reading field. One good piece of news that White Franklin had to share was that the "caravan" was now at Coram's Fields extending the teaching rooms by two. As usual the funding came from well-wishers and in this case monies were raised from the Jean Norton Trust Fund.[26] Mr and Mrs Norton and their friends and neighbours in Billericay provided not only "the caravan" (a terrapin) but also had it fitted out and modified. The site was small and at one point it looked as though the terrapin would have to be put in place by a helicopter but White Franklin helped by Mrs Cox and the foundling site trustees circumvented the problem. The new classrooms enabled the centre to have another teacher.

The bulletin articles were in the main from the staff of the centre or members of the Word Blind Committee. Macdonald Critchley had written a piece for Denis Williams' *Modern Trends in Neurology* and Williams allowed this to be reproduced in the bulletin. Critchley was so good at explaining dyslexia it seems important here to give a substantial summary of this article, "Some Observations Upon Developmental Dyslexia" as

---

26. The Jean Norton Trust Fund still exists. "It was founded in 1964 to provide help for children with dyslexia and support for training of teachers to deal with dyslexia".

it spells out clearly the hopes and fears of parents and teachers for their dyslexic children. He started by again visiting the problem of defining dyslexia by saying, "No adequate definition of specific dyslexia or developmental exists."

Neurologists, Critchley stated, had always viewed non-reading as a spectrum with "frank oligophrenics" (those intellectually disabled) at one end and seriously diturbed children at the other, and they knew there was a group at the centre of the spectrum of children with no other problems than that they just couldn't read, write and spell, and that these were "congenitally word-blind". Critchley emphasised that if a child of average intelligence couldn't read adequately he or she would suffer throughout their school life and because lacking in the ability to relate printed symbols to "the auditory properties of the words" he or she would be unlikely to spell adequately. Where other children overcame mistakes such as reversing letters the dyslexic child continued with those errors for longer and as a result boys, in particular, as they grew older, were likely to be disruptive.[27]

Critchley like most researchers in the field was aware of laterality and the preponderance of ambidexterity in dyslexic children and felt that there might be "minimal neurological deficits" resulting in "clumsy" children within this group, but that most grew out of this aspect of the syndrome. Similarly some dyslexics had difficulty with calculations but some just found it difficult to read the questions in maths. Poor readers with severe brain damage should be left out of equation Critchley suggested. He considered that parental and teacher attitudes played a huge part in a child coping with dyslexia. He described a child with a high IQ who overcame his early reading problems on his own and used Hendrick's definition "Ego Strength" to describe these young people, who Critchley felt became "ex-dyslexics" but allowed that they would always have atrocious spelling.

Unlike the much publicised stance of the early dyslexic movement Critchley did not think that children with a low IQ could not be dyslexic. He was concerned for those with average or above average intelligence

---

27.   It was thought there was only about one girl to five boys who were dyslexic.

because they underperformed which he and many others considered a waste. It was generally accepted that dyslexia was a familial disorder and as such some children would be dyslexics but also have low IQs. He was equally worried for these children as the prognosis educationally for them was not good.

Testing reading, Critchley pointed out, is a complex art. Some children could apparently read, even pronouncing the words correctly but without understanding and few 1960s reading tests involved comprehension. The existing tests did not allow for the amount of time taken to read. Critchley wrote of two standard dyslexic traits: to guess a word when reading or to insert a similar word. Another habit the dyslexic brain enjoys is to give a word of the opposite meaning. Critchley quoted "fast" for "slowly". However he noted, dyslexics only have a problem of understanding "verbal symbols" and not any other pictorial representation such as cars, birds, postage stamps or road signs and are often good at remembering faces.

Handwriting was another matter and Critchley had found that all the children he had worked with had a problem with it. The writing was usually poor and changeable but sometimes used to disguise spelling errors. The article ends abruptly with handwriting and his understanding of mirror images and he also commented on the use of "phonics patterns rather than established customs", capital letters in the middle of words, omissions and repetition of letters.

The Plowden Report had been published in 1967 and Gill Cotterell wrote a short, pithy summary of what was a huge publication. Plowden mentioned dyslexia only once and then briefly:

"Some of our witnesses have suggested the existence of specific developmental dyslexia (sometimes called word blindness), a failure in reading which is thought to be due to neurological causes. There are so many possible reasons for poor reading, such as late maturation, ill-timed or poor teaching, sensory and speech defects, strephosymbolia [misperceptions of letters or numbers which usually correct themselves in time] and the emotional disturbances which may both cause, and result from, retardation in reading, that it is difficult to be sure whether specific dyslexia exists as an independent factor. An acute difficulty in reading appears to be confined to a very small number of children, perhaps five or fewer in a thousand."[28]

It must have been disappointing to say the least for the centre for so little to be written about dyslexia when the committee and those working there were setting out to publicise the condition and they must have hoped that their findings and work would be taken more seriously. Plowden does go on to say:

"In the meantime, we are advised that if children have not learned to read by the age of nine they should be referred to an educational psychologist. If they are also clumsy runners, and unable to draw a diamond shape, a neurological examination is advisable. If possible the educational psychologist should come to the school and discuss the individual children with the teachers."[29]

This statement incensed Gill Cotterell as she felt untold damage would be done to a dyslexic child if he or she was left until age nine before they were considered, let alone diagnosed, with the syndrome. The rest of the article is an explanation of why dyslexic children should be recognised and helped as soon as possible.

Cotterell chose not to comment on the detail contained in the Plowden Report which covered all elements of education in primary schools in England and Wales in 1967 and particularly looked at the progress made since 1948. She does note that both boys' and girls' abilities in reading in 1967 were nearly a year-and-a-half ahead of what they had been in 1948. She also described the reported methods used in teaching young children how to read, all of which one would presume would be approved of by the centre, the message being that all methods should be considered depending on the needs of the individual. Perhaps it was Plowden's opinion that parents' attitudes to reading was of supreme importance and that this bore no relation to the parents' socio-economic place in society,

28. Plowden Report, *Children and Their Primary Schools*, 1967, p. 214. See, generally, see http://www.educationengland.org.uk/documents/plowden/
29. Ibid.

also that with children from "homes with a good literary background" this often meant that the parents had high expectations for their children. This might make the child anxious and cause long-term damage. One suspects that this was a swipe at middle-class families looking for reasons for their children not reading; the much talked of "middle-class disease".

Gill Cotterell and her colleagues were well aware of the gossip of the day which we are now not party to. Newspaper articles referred to dyslexia being a made-up excuse for lazy or stupid children. It is a pity that this coloured her attitude to the report, though maybe she also had limited space in which to air her opinions. Reading the Plowden Report now there is a lot of interesting information of the state of education at the time. The review ended with Cotterell asking why Plowden thought that gifted children should be recognised and helped as young as possible while dyslexic children should wait until they were nine before any action was taken.

Plowden:

"They [gifted children] may suffer from boredom and set up a habit of daydreaming and escaping." [30]

Cotterell:

"The gifted dyslexic will suffer acute anxiety at his failure too." [31]

In the 1967 bulletin, Vol. 2, while Cotterell was looking at Plowden Naidoo reviewed *Standards and Progress in Reading* by Joyce Morris and Tim Miles looked at "Reading Delay (Dyslexia) Final Report of a Survey" which was published in *The Health of the School Child 1964–1965*. Both Miles and Naidoo brought considerable intellectual rigour to their consideration of these articles and were scathing in their opinions of the findings. Naidoo sets the scene for the reader by explaining that *Standards and Progress in Reading* was the second half of an in-depth study of primary school children in Kent but that it was considered to be relevant

---

30. Ibid.
31. *Word Blind Committee Bulletin*, 1967, Vol. 2, No. 1, p. 11.

to children throughout the country. The National Foundation for Educational Research (NFER) published the second part of the study in 1966, the first half having been published in 1959 and it discussed, through the specifics of Kent children, the national situation of the "teaching of reading, school organization and the non-verbal ability in relation to standards and progress". The children studied, some 2,258 eight-to-ten-year-olds, were born in 1946 so the study was a long time in the making.

Naidoo noted that both whole word teaching and phonics were discussed but she felt the emphasis on whole word teaching rather than phonics led to a bias in favour of the former. As part of the report there was a further study concentrating on 714 children who were looked at again when they reached 14 and of that number 98 were designated "poor readers". Most of the findings were obvious, good readers came from what the report referred to as good schools and the "backward reader" tended to have emotional and behavioural problems, and the majority of these were boys.

Naidoo agreeing with Morris was horrified at how few poor readers were given remedial help within schools, only 15 children out of an initial group of 101 poor readers (98 made the final group). The reason for this was put down to the lack of specific training in working with children with reading difficulties in colleges of education. As for dyslexia, Morris found no evidence of the condition but, as Naidoo pointed out, she wasn't looking for it. School medical records, which were the source of basic information on the children, did not recognise the problem. Naidoo also argued with Morris' definition of dyslexia as a neurological problem:

"Morris recognises dyslexia as basically a 'neurological problem' and then appears to equate 'neurological problem' and 'brain defect'. Her definition of dyslexia as 'a reading disability due to organic brain defect' is wholly unacceptable."[32]

Naidoo rightly stated that at the time of writing it was impossible to know to what extent the dyslexic brain was different or damaged. She

---

32. *Word Blind Committee Bulletin*, 1967, Vol. 2. No. 1, p. 14.

felt it was wrong to use a word like "defect" which would suggest "damage" as it was usually obvious if a child was brain damaged. She accepted that there could be "neurological problems" but it was"misleading to regard neurological problems and organic brain defects as synonymous."

Morris thought that children with neurological problems were incapable of learning at all; this opinion was voiced at the conference on dyslexia in 1961. Naidoo knew the above to be false information and that with maturation all but the most severely dyslexic children improve even if not to their full potential. Naidoo finished the review with:

> "Unless the sample examined by Morris was a very unusual one indeed, there must have been within it at least a few dyslexic children. They were not sought for and therefore not found." [33]

Tim Miles was now reviewing the second section of a two part report (he had reviewed the first half in the first edition of the bulletin) and was no more impressed with the second half than he had been by the first, which was "the work of a luckless amateur". As the definitions used by that author, a principal school medical officer, were so lacking in precision Miles felt it made it impossible to "draw conclusions with confidence". He dissected the section and added his scientifically-based interpretation in the form of footnotes, which illustrated clearly its woolly nature. The poor author fell into a perfect trap by entitling his article "Reading Delay". Miles, with his colleagues, was endeavouring to bring awareness of the special nature of dyslexia to their audience.

> "But neither by derivation nor established usage does 'dyslexia' mean 'reading delay'; it describes the condition of a special group of delayed readers and spellers." [34]

Miles considered it necessary to have a special name for the children he and his colleagues were working with as only then would this group get the special care they needed. He likened dyslexia to tuberculosis and

---

33.   Ibid, p. 15.
34.   Ibid, p. 16.

suggested that it would be possible to refer to those with tuberculosis as "coughers" but this would not have the same effect as giving the condition its correct and scientific name. Miles being the kind man he was ends his roasting of the medical officer with:

> "If, however, the report convinces those in authority of the need for further research, then despite its shortcomings it will have done good." [35,]

By 1968, the work of the Word Blind Centre was well underway. The committee consisted of a prestigious mix: White Franklin, Critchley, Miles and Zangwill from the original group as was Miss Bird and Dr Kellmer Pringle, Director of the National Bureau for Co-operation in Child Care. A newcomer was Sir Wilfred Sheldon, Physician-Paediatrician to the Queen. All added breadth and gravitas.

In White Franklin's Foreword to the 1968 bulletin he welcomes Sandhya Naidoo as centre director recognising the work that she had already undertaken since 1966 when she first arrived. The research project, now in the hands of Naidoo, was realistically matching the research group to a norm group of children using age and type of school thereby making the project less complicated and above all possible.

The centre's waiting list was long which must have been of concern for all; even by taking on another teacher the it was still not able to deal with all who needed help. Ideally White Franklin wrote, there should be a Reading Centre in London, that could teach teachers and be a permanent place to work with children, a "workshop" for the teachers to practice in. In an ideal world this imagined centre would both assess children psychologically and physically so that the children in the "research laboratory" would fit the criteria set down by the centre. This dream would have called for a permanent centre and needed a permanent home and funding.

The Word Blind Centre was receiving feedback concerning the bulletin from parents who felt the journal was concentrating too much on the academic and technical side of the centre's work. In the 1968 bulletin

---

35.   Ibid, p. 16.

Kate Rackham put together a report on the actions taken by the centre and the ICAA in publicising dyslexia:

> "At the 1962 Conference 'wordblindness' and 'specific dyslexia' were completely unacceptable words. Since that time the words have passed into common usage and many leading national newspapers and periodicals as well as television have featured the problem."[36]

Rackham reported that during the year starting April 1966 there had been 598 enquiries to the ICAA's schools department each of which had been replied to personally and sometimes this had resulted in lengthy correspondence. The parents writing for help had been from all over the world as well as the UK: Libya, Zambia and Nepal were now added to the list. It was not always possible for the parents and professionals to visit the centre and help was given at a distance, and no child appears to have been sent away without some guidance. The pressure on the little unit must have been immense and to save the staff being over-burdened the bulletin was used as often as possible to pass on information and new ideas. Other inventive ways were also used to pass on the message. In 1967 a circular was sent to School Psychological Services explaining the work of the centre asking for details of any diagnosis and teaching help so that the centre would be able to pass this information on to enquirers. The feedback was positive and over 50 per cent replied in a friendly and helpful manner. All the details were painstakingly recorded in notebooks, no automatic entries into a computer in those days. The parents also had their own booklet *Guide to Parents* and the subscriber list for the bulletin stood at 554, over a third of which were sent overseas.

The 1966–67 annual report of the ICAA reported on the first Open Day for the centre. Families as well as teachers and educationalist attended. A success story was reported of an ex-pupil's good examination results. This was a product of the work undertaken with the student at the centre but also with the help of allowances given by examination boards for spelling errors and reading speed, fought for by the centre. Rackham was

---

36.   *Word Blind Committee Bulletin*, 1968, Vol. 2, No. 2, p. 35.

concerned to reassure readers of the bulletin that although the research and teaching for the research project was at the top of the list of priorities much else was being undertaken to support word-blind children.

In the same bulletin in the Foreword, White Franklin announced the new teachers' programme. The centre felt confident enough to offer teaching courses and the first 50 teachers were due to start a programme of talks and discussions in December 1968. The rest of his Foreword promoted articles on reports of conferences and work taking place in or as a result of the centre.

By 1968 Gill Cotterell had left the centre and was studying at Birmingham University. She was still in touch and contributed an article to the 1968 bulletin based on a paper about a group of non-readers who had been tested by that university when they were children (born 1942 to 1948). By the time Cotterell was working with them the men were aged between 16 and 22 (at the original testing they had been seven to 13). There was no suggestion that these young men were dyslexic. The study was to see how boys with reading problems had coped with life after school and what could be learnt about teaching and attitudes to non-readers. Their reading ages originally ranged from 5.4 to 8.4 years and their IQs from 75–127. The subjects were well-known to the research centre at Birmingham as most of the men had kept in touch. Cotterell had 27 subjects. They were tested with the normal battery of reading and spelling tests and she talked each man through an 82 point questionnaire writing the answers for him. All the subjects were underachieving and eight were semi-literate and, of the group, only one read for pleasure, although some read short newspaper articles and seven seldom read at all. Amazingly a few of the group had enjoyed school but, like the Cambridge research mentioned earlier, the larger proportion had a bad time especially at junior school.

The point of Cotterell's article was her long list of recommendations. Her frustration was apparent that more had not been done for these young men who, even so, had achieved a lot. Most were in work, but could have done so much better with help. Her basic appeal was for recognition, smaller teacher groups and sympathy.

White Franklin also contributed to the 1968 bulletin. He comes over as such a caring man, he was hugely busy and although he had a hand in so many projects he rooted for the dyslexia movement whenever he could. However he was not blinkered about it and was willing to accept that it was possible that they might not be able to prove the condition, not least because of its complexity. As a paediatrician he saw his and his colleague's roles as caring for the individual child while recognising this was difficult for the class teacher who had to consider the whole. He explained how he had come to realise that the symptoms being presented by his patients: vomiting, stomach pains, asthma-type symptoms were far from causing the child to be backward in reading, writing and spelling but were the results of an otherwise intelligent child being unable to cope with literacy. He thought educational psychologists were not seeing what he as a medical man was seeing. His opinion was that the tests being used by educational psychologists were too specific and didn't take into account the complex nature of the children being seen at the centre.

"Real difficulty follows when a child hears and sees but cannot make use of what he sees and hears. Intelligence, willpower, experience, memory or availability of previous impressions, degree of alertness, all pay their part. And the child must have the wish and the ability to co-operate. A failure of function in a test may depend on the severity of the defect, but it may also depend on the presence of several minor weaknesses or defects, or on an attitude of mind." [37]

At the centre a whole raft including professionals were used to look at each child: parents, teachers, educational psychologists as well as paediatricians so that this group could put together a detailed picture of a child. These findings were paired against norm groups of children who had no problems learning to read, write and spell but who were of comparable in age and intelligence. He is of course writing about the project being undertaken at the Word Blind Centre which would result in Sandhya Naidoo's report *Specific Dyslexia*.

---

37.   Ibid, p. 27.

White Franklin's hope was that the centre would be able to group together dyslexic children with similar problems and from the pattern of their difficulties put together teaching programmes suitable for each group. Extrapolated from this information would be the necessary teaching of the teachers to help such children. White Franklin knew ideally this should be undertaken in all schools but saw that it would have to start in centres such as the Word Blind Centre.

> "The earliest possible recognition and the best possible teaching methods, these are the aims of all who wish to help the dyslexic child." [38]

In the 1969 bulletin, matters had moved on apace. The research material for the project had been completed and the staff were busy putting the information together. The first teachers' course had happened and preparations were taking place for a meeting in February of 1969 to set up parents associations. The Foreword, probably by White Franklin, bemoaned the fact that teachers were not given literature about dyslexia as a result young children were not being identified at the first possible moment. This it was felt was due to the number of theories and cures being bandied about, making it possible for the "unbelievers" to deny the existence of dyslexia.

The most exciting move for the centre was the emergence of a national association for the parents of dyslexic children which would subsequently became the British Dyslexia Association. Several associations, near and far, had been formed over the years emanating from the conference in 1961, the most distant from London being in Scotland and Northern Ireland, closer to home North Kent but also Bath and Yorkshire. It was noticeable at the meeting in February 1969 that the associations were different from each other and had different needs but White Franklin could see that they would eventually group together as a whole. He had seen the same process of building an association with the families of cerebral palsied children. He wrote of the hopes and fears, of the anger and enthusiasm, but mostly how together they would be stronger than

---

38.   Ibid, p. 28.

staying as individual groups. By joining together it was easier to bring the "handicap" to the notice of the public and gain sympathy and support. Associations became centres for information and could call upon the services of experts. Through subscriptions it would be possible to set up assessment centres for research and teaching as well as funding, counselling and propaganda. He knew that at present teaching had to be undertaken outside of state schools but hoped that eventually this would be a "routine service' in all schools. However he considered that

> "what will then remain outside of the statutory services will be a Reading Centre for the conduct of research and the testing of new methods of prediction, assessment and teaching, and for revealing new problems and aspects of old ones."[39]

The 1972 bulletin saw the end of the Word Blind Centre and the contents have a definite end of an era feel to them. White Franklin and Naidoo closed the proceedings but the bulletin had to have some educational input and a B Allan contributed an article entitled "A Comparative Study of Progress Among Severely Dyslexic Children According to the Frequency of Lessons". As White Franklin "wrapped up" for the centre he listed its main achievements. First and foremost the forthcoming publication of the findings of their research in the shape of Naidoo's *Specific Dyslexia*. He acknowledged the recognition of dyslexia as seen in the list of conditions requiring special needs listed in the Chronically Sick and Disabled Persons Act 1970. Tim Miles had argued over the use of the word "acute" which is a medical term and therefore not applicable, but because dyslexia was on the list it was recognised and there was the possibility, or at least an expectation of, assistance from the state. Franklin was also excited about the formation of the British Dyslexia Association and handed the bulletin over to the North Surrey Dyslexia Society who had promised to carry on the good work and produce a journal.

The last year had produced two "teaching the teachers" conferences and resulted in *Assessment and Teaching of Dyslexic Children* first published in

---

39.   *Word Blind Committee Bulletin,* 1969, Vol. 2, No. 3, p. 54.

1970. Although dyslexia was still not fully recognised by the education authorities and colleges of education many ordinary teachers were coming forward for help and advice as they knew they had dyslexic children within their classes and wanted to help them.

Sandhya Naidoo's last article is a lovely mix of reminiscing about the centre, the children and the staff, and a summary of her report which was in the process of being published. Although she loved the centre's location as it was in the middle of London she and her fellow workers were at times exasperated by the bureaucracy involved just by being in Coram's Fields. The playground and buildings were locked-up long before the centre had finished working for the day, especially in winter. Often guests and workers alike were locked in or out. The 1966–1967 ICAA Annual Report talks of break-ins and vandalism which would have accounted for Naidoo's memories of having to bolt and bar doors and windows. Later still, bars were fitted to windows giving it a prison-like appearance from the outside, but nothing could diminish her love of the area and the place with its "hustle and bustle" atmosphere.

Naidoo in a summary of her final report writes of the in-depth analysis of each individual child and how this approach was the cornerstone of their work. Each child who came to the centre was minutely examined: physically, psychologically and educationally and this was the ethos of the centre, she stated yet again, thereby ruling out influences such as emotional disturbance, leaving just this thing called specific dyslexia. It was not that children who had other disabilities or who were not of average or above intelligence were not dyslexic but just that these factors detracted from the core problem. The intimate nature and environment of the centre helped in the process of analysis and all concerned were there to share and swap their experiences of each child. The centre did not think only intelligent children were dyslexic but the restraints of time and money meant they had to stick to one group.

The testing was simplified as much as possible but it still took a long time, three visits per child, taking up two-and-a-half days. This lengthy process was considered necessary both for the research but also so that the special tuition programme fitted each child exactly. The teaching methods were observed and reported so that the methods and findings could be part of the teaching the teachers programme. The 98 boys (see above) were split into two groups: reading retards and spelling retards (the language of the report not mine); the former were at least two years behind their chronological age (it should be noted that children of average or above average intelligence would be expected to read above their chronological age) and the second group were not so behind with reading but were handicapped by their inability to spell. It was hoped that through computer analysis other sub-groups would be found.

The teaching programmes that were tailor made for each child did work. The teachers used appropriate methods for each child who had differing problems and the teachers found that they had to rethink programmes as literacy milestones were achieved. It was necessary to keep the programmes fluid as well as structured. The teacher always had to put the child first so the work had to be interesting and the teacher had to be sympathetic and to listen:

"Our teachers had to adjust their teaching to the pupil's slow rate of learning while treating them as intelligent. Much over-learning is necessary."[40]

There were residual difficulties. The children learnt to read but tended to be "careless" readers and most continued to be poor spellers and with errors that were often particular to them. The teaching programmes continued until the they were at their chronological age in reading,

Specific Dyslexia is a detailed unbiased account not just of the research carried out at the centre but an overview of all the many articles the team used whilst reading around their subject. The book contains: tables, appendices, summaries and conclusions for the many educationalists and parents who were trying to understand their dyslexic children.

Naidoo's conclusion in her final article, however, was personal. She saw a discrepancy between a child's ability to learn in general from the specific problem of reading, writing and spelling as hugely important. She considered that dyslexia was not just a reading difficulty but "a disorder of learning to read, write and spell", that literacy difficulties were only

40. Sandhya. Naidoo, "Reminiscences of the Word Blind Centre", *The Word Blind Bulletin*, 1972, Vol. 2, No. 4, p. 69.

part of the condition and that most dyslexics had other minor problems like speech defects, problems with laterality and poor sound discrimination. However these issues did not and do not form regular patterns and emotional problem might also be present. Difficulties with reading, writing and spelling often resulted in emotional upheaval. Finally, Naidoo added that some of their dyslexics had a family history of reading difficulties, some may have had minor brain defects and there could also be a mixture of both.

Many newspaper articles were written about the last conference and about the report when it was later published but they did not say anything new and in the main just delivered a summary of Naidoo's project report. However, viewed from the distance of decades there was not the same animosity shown at the end of the life of the centre as there had been at the original conference in 1961. Ten years had changed public opinion. Dyslexia and the term word-blind were now mainly accepted although the syndrome was far from being recognised. Naidoo's down to earth attitude must have helped.

In 1971 the Word Blind Centre closed. Naidoo and her team were too honest to say they had all the answers but from their small study they had learnt a lot and *Specific Dyslexia* became the bible for most people working in the field. It lays out a clear working model of the testing and assessment necessary to come to a conclusion as to whether a child has specific literacy problems as opposed to a general learning problem.

From Percy to Peter

CHAPTER SEVEN

A Taste of Research at the Time of the Word Blind Centre

The bulletin published articles by those working at the centre but was also a voice for others researching dyslexia. As seen in previous chapters, those groups working on dyslexia tended to be isolated, so work by ophthalmologists was reported in their journals, others in the *British Medical Journal* and so on. It was hoped that the *Invalid Children's Aid Association Bulletin* would reach all supporters of dyslexic children. White Franklin wrote in the Foreword to the 1966 edition that it was:

"intended to carry to the interested public, as well as professional people, ideas and views about dyslexia and word blindness. The articles express the opinions of the various authors but are definitely not edited nor selected to fit any pattern. Nor is the content of the articles guaranteed in any way either by the editor or, still less, by the members of the Word Blind Committee."[1]

Ophthalmologists feature strongly in the dyslexia story so it wasn't surprising to find an article by E A Knight in the second edition of the bulletin.[2] The boy Knight was working with was 12 at the time of testing and had normal sight but was not reading and considered by his school to be inattentive and "stupid". It did not help "Master S" that he was good at arithmetic as this convinced his teachers that he was just lazy in other subjects. It was amazing, even in 1963, that his teachers had reacted in this way as S's problems in reading were extreme. He could name the entire alphabet and read small words but, even with small words, when

---

1. *Word Blind Committee Bulletin*, Vol. 1.
2. Ibid, Vol. 1, No. 2, October 1963 (originally printed in *The Optician*, June 7th 1963).

writing he would get the letters in the wrong order. Luckily for S his parents persevered and sent him to a psychiatrist who after a few simple tests declared him to have specific developmental dyslexia. S's mother was distraught about her son as he was so demoralised and considered that he was a fool and would never be able to learn. The headmaster to his credit recommended a complete report on S although he had only seen one other case in 30 years of teaching. Knight finished his article by saying he felt he and his fellow ophthalmologists would find other cases similar to S's and that as part of their investigations they should ask about the child's academic record.

During Bannatyne's reign, Alan Gorton wrote for the bulletin. He was an educational psychologist for Dewsbury Education Committee and observed that dyslexic children (he termed the condition "specific dyslexia") showed several symptoms other than a difficulty in reading and spelling. Literacy is always the most quoted problem for a dyslexic person but the "soft symptoms" as Critchley called them were and are as bothersome as the difficulties with literacy. Gorton listed six areas to be aware of: speech defects or delay, right-left disorientation, weak sequencing skills, emotional problems brought on by not reading, hyperactivity, and a family history of specific dyslexia. His theory was that if a child shows four or more of these symptoms he or she would in all probability be dyslexic.

He undertook a research programme drawing on children aged nine to ten years from randomly chosen schools in his LEA; 694 children were given reading tests and from these 100 were selected as being below the expected norm for their age range. The 100 were then given a battery of tests including a questionnaire looking at the six symptoms noted above. Fourteen showed five out of the six. "Specialist peripatetic teachers" then gave all 100 children help with their reading and after two years the children were re-tested. They all improved except for 14. Gorton concluded:

"This emphasises two points, first that specific dyslexic children appear resistant to available methods and techniques in remedial teaching, and second that this area is in need of study."[3]

Gorton's findings fitted in well with the ethos of the Word Blind Centre but it can be ascertained from this article that there were other research programmes besides the work at the centre taking place at the time.

Some of the material published appeared somewhat wacky but presumably the sub-committee overseeing the publication thought it was fair for allcomers to have a say. Miss B Kettlewell, a teacher with Hertfordshire, wrote an article in two parts. Firstly a definitive statement about laterality:

"The truly left handed person would tend to use his left hand for writing and to reproduce the visual memories from the right hemisphere, focusing so that the reading matter falls mainly on the right halves of both eyes. He stores and reproduces mirror images (Orton, 1937) and may start reading and writing on the right side of the page, producing mirror writing."

She goes on to say that, more often, the dyslexic child has mixed dominance. Kettlewell also had an interesting theory that Europeans were naturally right-handed so produced writing from left to right whilst "Arabic, which is written from right to left, was probably evolved by a left-handed race".

Most of Kettlewell's article looks at the importance of optical dominance and she backs up her theories with research evidence. However she had not read Orton when she started her work, research for a PhD, and in retrospect she found she agreed with him in many areas. How could she not do so considering the volume of research Orton and his colleagues undertook and the number of children they were able to observe? Although by the 1960s a lot of Orton's work had been overtaken by the then current research, his observations of mirror writing and how dyslexics muddle letters and sounds stood the test of time making his

---

3.   Alan Gorton, "The Incidence of Specific Dyslexia", *Word Blind Committee Bulletin*, June 1964, Vol. 1, No. 3, pp. 6–7.

complicated and difficult term for dyslexia "strephosymbolia"[4] relevant. Kettlewell like many people writing on the subject of dyslexia finishes her article by wishing that children with a predisposition to dyslexia could be sorted out at a young age and thereby given multi-sensory teaching as early as possible.

T T S Ingram worked with children in Scotland and had come into contact with dyslexics. He was happy in his article "The Dyslexic Child" to use the term dyslexia. He was clear that many children suffered from a form of dyslexia and dysgraphia and made "poor progress" in all subjects but that only children who have difficulties with reading, writing and spelling but "who do not show backwardness in other school subjects" can be referred to as specific dyslexics. Ingram considered that the terms "word-blind", "developmental dyslexia" and "specific developmental dyslexia" should all come under the term specific dyslexia.

Like Kettlewell, Ingram felt that the anxiety caused by not reading was the main reason that the dyslexic child shows signs of emotional behaviour, especially as it often took at least three years, if not a lot longer, for dyslexia to be identified. Whatever different perspectives the researchers came from they all cited anxiety as a problem and early diagnosis as a necessity. Ingram suggested a list of procedures that would aid a dyslexic child including referral to a child guidance clinic, but he was in sorrow that few children would be identified, never mind treated. He was mortified by how the average teacher in the 1960s was not aware of the individual child's abilities in literacy and put this down in some respect to bright children hiding their disabilities, but also to the reluctance of teachers to admit their pupils' difficulties, seeing this as a slur on their teaching ability.

Like many in the early days of the centre Ingram was saddened by educational psychologist's attitude to dyslexics. He wrote that many would not ask for medical assistance and at times misdiagnosed mild cerebral palsy for dyslexia while others refused to admit the existence of dyslexia and attributed non-reading to poor teaching, emotional problems and

---

4.   "A delay or difficulty in learning to read which is out of harmony with a child's general intellectual ability. At the outset it is characterised by confusion between similarly formed but oppositely oriented letters, and a tendency to changing order of direction in reading": Samuel T Orton, *Reading Writing and Speech Problems in Children*, 1937, W W Norton, New York.

"mental retardation". The result of the lack of help within the school situation was that children were presented to GPs with a myriad of physical and mental health problems all stemming from their problems with literacy but of course finding the cause of a child's behaviour took some unpicking.

Equally, Ingram advised his readers to test all the more obvious reasons for not reading before concentrating on dyslexia. But he advised that if there was a history of literacy problems within the child's immediate and extended family then they were almost certainly dyslexic. Like Kettlewood, Ingram saw a connection between children who were either ambidextrous or who had a variable dominant eye and problems with reading.[5] He also noted that children who in the early years muddle sounds and words may also indicate the presence of dyslexia.

Geoffrey Sceats a former headmaster from New Zealand contributed several articles to the bulletin and in "Report of a Case-Study of a Ten-Year-Old Non-Reader" and "A Technique of Developing Conscious Awareness of Laterality and General Orientation in Space" he too concentrated on laterality and the necessity for the child to be able to orientate himself or herself in any given space before he or she could even contemplate learning to read.

A child needs to know which is up and down, left and right, and so on. Sceats gave a detailed case history of a ten-year-old boy, Arthur, presenting with a high IQ but whose reading and spelling were at a low level. Arthur was taught some words using a Fernald phonic programme but his progress was slow and inconsistent. After more tests Sceats realised that the boy had no sense of direction and therefore found it impossible to remember the sounds of letters that need orientation such as b/d and p/q. He developed a practical method of teaching Arthur left, right, up, down, in and out and reinforced this routine regularly for short periods of time throughout the day employing his parents to carry this on out of school. After eleven days Arthur had learnt his left from his right:

---

5.   Ingram quoted Margaret Macmeeken.

"Eleven days later he knew that he knew, announcing 'I know right from left now. Try me' and he was correct."[6]

Once Arthur had established directionality and with the help of other detailed phonic-based reading programmes he progressed and even after holidays from studying he remembered what he had learnt and became a positive learner. In Sceats' second article he gives a detailed programme with diagrams of how to teach directionality to a child who does not have this natural ability.

In the winter of 1966, the bulletin was full of helpful articles including one from Violet Spraings, "The Dyslexias—A Psycho-Educational and Physiological Approach". Spraings was the director of psychological and educational studies at a unit for cerebral palsied children in Northern California and she and Douglas Crowther had undertaken a study of 45 dyslexic children. The article is an in-depth list of the tests undertaken and the results found. It is doubtful whether the checklist of symptoms has ever been bettered; covering not only literacy and IQ tests but also family background and the emotional effects on non-readers. Her definition of dyslexia also takes some beating, remembering of course the constraints of scientific knowledge of the day and no MRI scans:

"Dyslexia is a symbolic language disorder, with a somewhat characteristic syndrome, where there is a poor ability to learn to interpret and retain the symbols needed for reading in the absence of major mental defect, major perceptual aberration, and where the child has been exposed to an organized attempt to teach him to read over a minimum period of a year."[7]

Sprainge reminded her readers of the difficulty in testing dyslexics because of their problems with language and advised testing with the WISc rather than Stanford Binet because of the latter relying heavily on verbal skills. Sprainge and Crowther came to the conclusion that there were three types of dyslexia: visual where the child is unable to learn

6. Geoffrey J Sceats MA, "Report of a Case-Study of a Ten-Year-Old Non-Reader", *Word Blind Committee Bulletin*, June 1964, Vol. 1, No. 3, pp. 4–6.
7. Violet Spraings, "The Dyslexias—A Psycho-Educational and Physiological Approach", *Word Blind Committee Bulletin*, Winter 1966, Vol. 1, Nos. 6 and 7, pp. 32–36.

the shape of letters' "appearance"; auditory where the child is unable to learn the sounds of letters; and "visuo-auditory" a mixture of the first two. A fourth group was possible but Sprainge was still working on this concept at the time of the article.

In the 1969 bulletin, the Word Blind Committee were allowed to print an article by Professor J W Tibble who had given a lecture at the Annual General Meeting of the ICAA on "Education and Learning". It was relevant to the 1960s thinking on the child's place in the whole business of education. Historically, Tibble wrote, the child was seen as "a receptacle" and the educator imprinted information on to a blank format. The child was passive in this process with the teacher and parents "shaping, directing, controlling and disciplining". By the beginning of the twentieth century thinking had "fashionably" swung to the child being like other animals that learn instinctively. Tibble acknowledged that children learn through play but seemed less convinced by the teacher as a conductor who attempts to direct play. He saw the external influences of both education and society and the natural learning ability of the child as being an "adjustment".

> "Learning is seen as a process of adjusting to these influences, of finding out how to fit in, acquire skills and knowledge valued by the society in question, control impulses not so approved and so on."[8]

Tibble preferred the term "assimilation", meaning that it is important for the child to come to terms with his or her situation to understand it and be happy with it. Outside influences, society, were needed to teach the child acceptable behaviour. When education is added to the mix the child needs to be able to acquire techniques, information and understanding at the level applicable to their age and intelligence. If however there is a defect in this process, whatever that might be, the child is liable to fail and this failure will become accumulative. If help is given and the means of teaching widened the child can again achieve. It is easy to understand how important this lecture was to the Word Blind Committee.

---

8. Professor J W Tibble (Emeritus Professor of Education, Leicester University), "Education and Learning", *Word Blind Committee Bulletin*, 1969, Vol. 2, No. 3, pp. 44–45.

er part of this article encouraged the use of the arts as a means
ıg for all "handicapped" children. Two reasons: one that less
is placed on a child undertaking arts projects; and two the
child is more able to grow though different forms of art. This approach
mirrored the techniques used by Edouard Seguin and later Montessori.

In August 1968, Naidoo found time in her busy schedule to attend
an international conference in Copenhagen the Second World Congress
on Reading. She noted that the majority of participants, as would be
expected, came from the USA and Scandinavia with only a few from the
UK. She recognised that a conference on reading held in the UK was to
take place two weeks hence. The lectures were about general concerns
with literacy and it was proposed that a World Literacy Day take place on
the 8ᵗʰ September each year. By 1968, in fact, World Literacy Day was up
and running, the inception was announced by UNESCO on November
17, 1965 and first celebrated in 1966 (and it is still taking place).[9]

Naidoo was particularly interested in a programme in Northern Thai-
land to help tribe members to read. One method being used was to write
messages on headbands worn by the girls from the villages which encouraged the boys to learn them. Would this be reported in the twenty-first
century? On a more sensible note, she reported a study into reading speed
and how Professor A J Harris noticed that readers tended to adopt the
same speed of writing for all tasks where differing speeds would be more
efficient. It was felt that a speed of 800–900 words per minute was probably the maximum if comprehension was to be maintained.

The lectures Naidoo must have been waiting for were by Professors
Vernon and Preston on dyslexia. Vernon was an old friend of the Word
Blind Centre and Preston from the USA. These reinforced the findings
of the centre including the conclusion that although heredity and maturational lag were causal factors, brain damage wasn't. Preston did feel
that if "dyslexia-inclined" children could be identified at an early age it
would be possible to teach out many of the reading and spelling problems felt by many of them.

9.　See https://en.unesco.org/commemorations/literacyday

By 1969 the research at the centre had moved on at such a pace that it was being talked about at other national conferences. The bulletin reported through an article by a former teacher at the centre, Mrs B Allen on a lecture given by Dr Kellmer Pringle and Mrs Mason. Kellmer Pringle was, of course, one of the committee members of the centre and she and Mrs Mason had made a study of children with speech difficulties published as *Reading and Writing Difficulties in Childhood.*[10] Their work was based on a study in Scotland and bears out all the findings and work being undertaken at the centre. The central argument of the lecture was that "deprived" children and dyslexic children showed marked similarities in an inability to acquire literacy skills. The term "deprived" will have referred to emotionally and socially deprived children. The deprived children studied had not established the required levels of vocabulary and social interaction necessary to be able to read. The other half of the study looked at dyslexic children and showed that both were held back by their respective problems. The up side of the findings was that the educational methods being developed for dyslexic children were found to be helpful for "deprived" children. Mrs Mason noted that late speakers nearly all went on to have reading difficulties.

Although the work of the centre revolved around the convoluted issues of dyslexia, other researchers concentrated only on reading. Educators today are aware of the complexity of acquiring the skill of reading but it was a fairly new area of study in the 1960s. Mrs Allen also reported on other talks concerning reading research. Dr Samuel Weintraub particularly highlighted the need for a child to be able to split a word into syllables but also to be able to fuse the parts together again to form a word, and that this did not always happen automatically. Ruth Strang (another researcher well-known to the centre) had observed, as did the workers at the centre, that a teacher's observations of a child were so important. Strang encouraged her listeners to study how their children learnt to read, this would assist not only the child in question but, by understanding the individual, help the many. She encouraged teachers to believe in their children; quoting the work of the centre she reported

---

10. *Journal of Child Care in General Practice,* 1965.

that this was what they did best, that they believed their children would read given the necessary tools an, even with small gains, children would prosper.

Before the advent of the internet Mrs Allen saw conferences as a good place to form connections and the coffee and lunch breaks of the Fifth Annual Study Conference of the United Kingdom Reading Association had proved to be the perfect venue for networking. This sideways look at the other work in progress in the early-1970s brings this story back to the Word Blind Centre, the final conference and its winding-up.

CHAPTER EIGHT

The Final Conference

By 1971 the Word Blind Centre had closed and the remaining pupils were moved to the Ebury Road Centre, Victoria, London. In January 1972, prior to the publication of the research report *Specific Dyslexia*, the ICAA instigated a conference to discuss the work of the centre. Two teaching conferences had already taken place, resulting in the publication of *Assessment and Teaching Dyslexic Children*. These books combined to become the basis of much of the work undertaken subsequently by the dyslexic movement.

It is worth remembering the time when these publications appeared and to note how clear and unbiased the works were in the face of the criticism and antagonism the dyslexia movement had engendered. It is also interesting to observe how, in writing about the history of dyslexia in 1971, there is a subtle change as the authors have a more in-depth understanding of their topic. Although the climate of the time was still somewhat anti-dyslexia, those within the movement were sure of their ground and knew in which direction they should be moving.

Alfred White Franklin gave the opening lecture of the 1972 conference as he had at the first one in 1961. The conference, "Dyslexia Where Now?" was hosted by the ICAA and there were 130 delegates. By 1972 White Franklin had retired from the ICAA but was still active in striving to help problem children and in particular those with dyslexia. To help the audience White Franklin asked questions: Did dyslexia exist? Had the Word Blind Centre provided profiles that could be used to identify a dyslexic at six-years-old, and had an appropriate screening test been invented? He went on to ask whether the centre had provided a suitable teaching programme or acted as a meeting place for doctors, teachers and

173

psychologists to exchange information? Had it acted as a link between university research centres? He acknowledged there had been a duty of care to the children who had been selected for research and to the trusts that provided the funding for the centre and research, and he saw the centre as a vehicle to gain the public's interest in dyslexia.

Pausing in his questioning, he admitted that originally the centre had veered away from giving an exact definition of dyslexia as it had felt this would have taken up too much time and effort (the centre's time had always been limited), however he felt this had proved to be a bad decision. He saw that a definition *was* required by the public and he cited the then recently aired current affairs programme *Man Alive* that had spent virtually the whole time discussing "words and definitions" and not actually reached the important message about dyslexia.

White Franklin set out the research programme and explained how the centre had chosen a group of children as their subjects who were ready to learn and had the ability to learn, who were of "average" or "above average" intelligence. This, unfortunately, had led to the public perception that the centre considered that only such children could be dyslexic and he wanted to lay the ghost of that falsehood. The Word Blind Committee had always known that dyslexia might be found in any child but in trying to unravel a difficult problem they had chosen to use a group they felt would most benefit from their work. The problem covered all groups of children including those with emotional problems. The centre had looked at the problems caused by dyslexia and as a result had provided coaching in coping skills.

White Franklin's regret was that, unfortunately, the team had not found a suitable screening test for six-year-olds, but those in the field continued to observe the tests in use both in the UK and the USA. He felt that a screening test for children on entering school would be the "biggest advance in the management of reading difficulties."

Dyslexia had caught public interest through the original conference in 1961 and articles in the bulletins. The media had also played a part and most of the exposure had been positive. By 1972 dyslexia had been included ("acute dyslexia") in an Act of Parliament, but White Franklin was much exercised by the *Man Alive* programme which had only taken place two weeks previously and he implied that because of it the general public would now recognise the term dyslexia.

He used the opportunity, through the conference, to praise the educationalist Joyce Morris who in 1972 was still against what she saw as the elitism of dyslexia, although in time her attitude changed. He acknowledged her work in the field of general literacy difficulties and emphasised that the two groups, those working with dyslexics and those with all non-readers, should work together not against each other as they were all striving for the same thing. By highlighting the needs of dyslexics this would shine a light on all children who needed help with literacy. He was not in the blame game but felt that if there was fault it should be laid at the feet of the Department for Education and the teacher training colleges (colleges of education) for not putting enough emphasis on reading difficulties in general. He hoped that the new National Association for Dyslexics would make friends with educational psychologists. Disagreements had started at the 1961 conference, however by 1972 educational psychologists were accepting that not all slow readers were non-readers for the same reason. White Franklin pointed out that children with emotional problems could be disturbed because they were having problems reading rather than because they were disturbed.

Educational psychologists had started calling the condition "specific learning difficulties" which was accepted by White Franklin who saw the wisdom in them not being too definite in their terminology. He wanted his colleagues (paediatricians) to work together with as many educational psychologists as possible. Again he emphasised the need to alter the perception that dyslexics came from only one social class, with no other disability, and no other conditions other than dyslexia. The centre had selected the research group from one socio-economic group with no other problems just as a tool to try and get a handle on the whole twisted issue of dyslexia. Neurologists had been accused of empire building and of "stepping on the toes" of educational psychologists. This he felt was probably the fault of the neurologists and that they would quickly step out of the way once a reasonable battery of tests had been put together, thereby leaving educational psychologists to do their own work. His continuing worry was that by not giving the condition a name it was difficult to assess the prevalence of the problem. However from the research being undertaken into all non-readers there was a possibility 15 per cent of six-to-nine-year-olds were not reading (excluding the "subnormal"). The numbers of children not reading in the UK in the early-1970s was scary and he considered a good proportion could be dyslexic, and as a result he saw the absolute necessity to improve the teaching of reading in primary schools and to set up screening programmes.

Centre stage then moved to the people who had the day-to-day running of the Word Blind Centre. The first speaker was Kate Rackham (schools' secretary, ICAA) and she openly admitted that her job was nothing like the position she thought she had originally undertaken. At That time she had seen the job as organizing fees from LEAs (particularly Inner London LEA) and sending out material to professionals, but it quickly became much more. As an example, she read a letter from a distraught mother with two boys who had dyslexic problems but for whom there had been no help. It was representative of hundreds received by the centre.

At the outset she saw her task as attempting to minimise publicity at least until the research was complete, but she and the other staff had a "rude awakening" when they realised right from the beginning the extent of the interest engendered. They had not anticipated the frustration and distress of parents and teachers of dyslexic children. Every time an article appeared in the press there would be piles of letters, in 1966–67 there were 598 and half of these were from parents. By 1970 after an article in *The Times* the staff of the centre had thought ahead and arranged for many of the letters to go directly to emerging local organizations. Also Sandhya Naidoo produced a "guide to parents" that gave guidelines for parents to follow and this helped Rackham and her team as they now had something to give to worried parents. The centre tried to bat enquiries and worries back to local authorities and although this worked to some extent in a lot of cases the help given by the LEAs was inadequate.

As the years progressed and in some cases, although the child was assessed and a programme of work organized by the centre, the child could not attend there because of where they lived. In the London Metropolitan Archive is a handwritten register dated "1/1/67" on which are the locations of the children either helped at the centre or seen by and advised by it. They came from far and wide. The obvious questions asked were: where to go for help and what schools recognise the problem? At first the answer was "nowhere" but, as the centre progressed and offered teaching courses, more teachers were prepared to take on children in their own areas, but the numbers were still small, few and far between. Some schools offered to help but without really understanding the problem or being able to offer the right type of help. The staff at the centre were devastated to realise that in some cases they just could not help.

Rackham noted that by late in the life of the centre the easiest cases were being dealt with locally leaving the centre with the difficult and complex ones, but what was going to happen now? While the centre existed there was help available but without it and with the day-to-day support removed, help could slip back to the pre-centre position. In an attempt to bridge the gap, centre staff had pulled together a geographical index to put dyslexics and teachers in touch with each other, but it was "sketchy" as there had not been enough time to do a good job. Of course, all of the work involved in a teacher/pupil index would have been undertaken by hand using a card index system, little cards filled out by a secretary and filed alphabetically in a small plastic box, no copies, and no computers.

Rackham returned to the subject of letters. Were those from parents "hysterical rants"? Rackham thought not, a few were hysterical but most showed an intelligent, rational attitude to their child's problem, and so when there was an overwrought anxious parent they stood out from the many. The facts tended to speak for themselves. The centre tried to listen to worried parents giving them time, and found that even half-an-hour listening helped greatly, either to answer questions or to spur the parent to keep on trying.

In conclusion, she returned to the children and quoted a boy who was so difficult he had been placed by his school in a "retarded" group but with help from the centre he was now "a joy to teach" and well on the way to taking a science degree. She thought that workers in the field had to be realistic and help dyslexic children to achieve the best practical life they could manage. For some this would be attaining an academic career despite their disability but for others it would be giving them the confidence to get around their problems and achieve a good life even if that meant drawing a diagram rather than writing an essay. Her motto was "nothing succeeds like success".

Sandhya Naidoo gave a précis of the work which led up to the research project and an outline of the research which resulted in the report *Specific Dyslexia*. Typical perhaps of a scientist, she stated honestly that she did not want to go into detailed aspects of the research prior to publication. Like White Franklin, she was to lay the myths around the dyslexia movement. In particular that those involved in the Word Blind Centre were only interested in middle-class children, as the committee had always known dyslexia occurred in all social groups, at all levels of intelligence and in all ethnic groups. By limiting the research to 98 boys from one socio-economic group and of roughly the same intelligence they had hoped to isolate dyslexia and not muddy the waters with other factors affecting the boys' reading abilities. What they proved was that, whatever the variations in symptoms, the condition was within the child and not influenced by external factors.

Naidoo spoke movingly of how important all participants were in the task undertaken by the centre. The research programme was led by assessment and the teaching was experimental, innovative and flexible but also tightly observed and recorded. The teachers looked for reactions, responses and progress and these were fed back to the medical/psychological team giving them greater insight into the condition. As a result Naidoo could not state strongly enough how important was the interdisciplinary nature of the centre.

The messages given by Naidoo and White Franklin was repeated many times, in the bulletin, in *Specific Dyslexia* and at the 1972 conference. The picture that emerged from the research was not of one syndrome but two main groups. One group, the worst affected, had profound difficulties with reading, spelling and writing, the other could learn to read but were usually late doing so and read inaccurately but found spelling and therefore writing extremely difficult. Naidoo was well aware of the worldwide research projects and felt it would have been surprising if they had found only one outcome considering research taking place in the UK and USA. Through observing how their children learned, the group became aware of how complex were the skills required to read, write and spell. The commonest symptom shown had been the marked unevenness in development, this could be seen in a dyslexic child even before he or she began to learn to read.

In conclusion she felt it was imperative that a centre funded by government be set up to carry on the work of the Word Blind Centre. She considered it to be of utmost importance that all children who fell into the two groups (those who could not read or spell and those who could read but not spell) should be investigated for possible specific dyslexia. The value of an interdisciplinary approach was underlined by the chief medical officer in his report to the Secretary of State for Education on the health of the schoolchild 1966–68. Finally Naidoo felt that there was a necessity to identify the dyslexic child as when he or she was as young as possible, before they became frustrated and depressed and she reminded her audience that every child's right to an education commensurate with his needs was laid down in the 1944 Education Act, i.e. there was a statutory public obligation to provide every child with an education according to age, ability and aptitude.[1] For a lucky few, dyslexic children were educated according to their age and disability rather than their potential. They needed diagnosis and remedial teaching and an education that allowed them to fulfil that potential, otherwise teachers had failed in its duty.

The remaining speaker was Gill Cotterell. She with Sandhya Naidoo had played a large part in the teaching conferences which resulted in the report *Assessment and Teaching of Dyslexic Children*. Cotterell outlined her time at the centre and thanked the ICAA for giving her the opportunity to undertake it, from which she personally had learnt a huge amount. She was still astounded by the number of intelligent children who had every opportunity to read but could not. She had seen the frustrations for student and teacher alike at having to work at such a slow pace and for the teacher the struggle to make the teaching interesting enough to keep a bright child's attention. She knew that a teacher could never presume

---

1.   Sandhya Naidoo, "Dyslexia Where Now?", 1972.

that the dyslexic child understood any aspect of literacy unless he or she personally had taught it to them. Cotterell had seen how complicated the sound/image relationship was for these children and as a result realised why they did not succeed in the average classroom.

The word "acute" used in the 1970 Education Act worried the professionals as it was not accurate in an educational or medical sense, but Cotterell nonetheless decided to pick up the word and use it. What did "acute" mean to her: a child who despite all positive teaching and a settled home-life couldn't read. A child with mild dyslexia who if undiagnosed would in time have real problems. A child who was a non-starter because bad spelling left them ill-equipped to cope with normal school life. She had seen young teenagers referred to the centre as medical referrals because of behavioural problems and that these symptoms disappeared when given special help with reading and writing. She had seen how this particular group often slipped through the net as they could apparently cope but their spelling let them down.

The final part of the 1972 conference was given over to questions and answers and here we see how far the movement had changed over the ten years. The Q & A session was bound to be a difficult ride, and although the centre team did not have all the answers they did have experience. They still didn't know exactly what dyslexia was but they had all seen what effect it had on children. It would take until the science of the brain had developed for computer imaging to actually see into the brain, but the effects of the disorder were there in front of any of these workers who had spent more than half-an-hour with a dyslexic child. The children seen at the centre should all have been reading and spelling with some competence but they weren't.

The first question from the floor was, perhaps predictably, "Is there such a thing as dyslexia?" and as always the answer was "Yes". The observations had shown that given a child with all the opportunities their children had they should have been reading, even if the progress was slow it was progress, but with dyslexic children if they were not taught in a multi-sensory manner they did not improve.

The questions then moved to the research around the 98 boys although the centre had seen and taught many more children than this. First:

did the research group examine the control group and find little or no abnormalities? Naidoo answered that they looked for oddities frequently seen among the dyslexic children being taught at the centre and these differences weren't seen as much in the control group.

> "[S]tatistics were showing significant differences between experimental and control groups so far as minor neurological dysfunctions were concerned."[2]

White Franklin and a Dr Holt (not Maisie Holt) batted about "testing", psychologists and neurologists coming at the child from different angles. The neurologist looked for the abnormal, the psychologist looked at skills and measured them against "established standards". Different approaches, but looking for information leading to "the working of the child's brain and nervous system".

The questions moved to practical matters, particularly examinations. Even at this early stage in the history of the modern dyslexic movement it was recognised that dyslexics were at a disadvantage when taking examinations and already the examination boards were allowing questions to be read and tape-recorders to be used and the term "special provisions" was coined as the acceptable one for the needs of dyslexic candidates. That question led to another concern, competition for dyslexic children was it a good or bad thing?

Mrs Bradshaw spoke of a child who had failed in a competitive environment and had to be taught to understand his failure and to use it as a tool and this would help anxiety. Sandhya Naidoo said competition, because of failure, could cause anxiety. Most dyslexics especially the intelligent ones were aware of their problems even from as young as six years and where there was no external pressure and in the most supportive environment the child could feel failure, so placing him or her in a competitive situation could do nothing but harm and it wasn't surprising that so many dyslexics presented as disturbed. It was not possible to remove the inner pressure but it was possible to remove the external pressure.

---

2.   Ibid.

The audience recognised the need for teaching courses and some provision had been made for more of them through the emergent Dyslexia Association which started with the North Surrey Group. Mrs Welchman said that the LEAs were being helpful by paying for the courses. Helen Arkell had also started teaching courses in Fulham. They all felt that the training colleges should be covering remedial teaching. Birmingham was quoted as having a remedial unit though the training did not necessarily cover the type of multi-sensory methods that were necessary for dyslexics. White Franklin noted that training was in the process of being improved. Until the 1960s it was presumed that most just learnt to read without teaching and that it would take time for the new ideas to filter through the system and be accepted by the colleges.

The questions swung back to the definition of dyslexia. Sandhya Naidoo felt it was misleading for critics to insist on a narrow definition and that it was not necessary to have a constant set of characteristics arising from a single cause. Dyslexia was a problem with encoding and decoding language, and dysphasia was used to describe a difficulty with speech and language, but in both cases there was something additional. She explained that children who couldn't read because they had not been given the opportunity to learn to read could not be called dyslexic. Dyslexia has something to do with the way a child matures and it could be genetic or organic, and from the research they had found it could also be neurological or a perinatal abnormality.

"There is no single factor giving rise to the disability but the possibility of several".[3]

Naidoo said that a teacher trained at Birmingham or Reading, or any remedial teacher, could teach a dyslexic child if they understood the child's particular problems. The methods used were not so different to those used for other backward readers, but the teacher had to accept that the dyslexic child takes a long while to learn to read, longer than normal and that they would have particular problems with spelling. The key in

---

3.   Ibid.

designing a programme of learning was allowing for an uneven pattern of development which probably dated back to early childhood. Naidoo would allow that research at the Word Blind Centre and in America showed that if there was a characteristic it was the inability to sequence both sounds and shapes.

Oliver Zangwill joined in at this point with down-to-earth common sense. If anyone needed to know what dyslexia was they should sit down with a dyslexic child and try to teach him or her to spell. It was pointless to keep looking for a definition; they all knew the condition existed and that it is necessary to help the children who suffer from it. Zangwill emphasised the importance of moving ahead with the knowledge and experience which by then existed.

Alfred White Franklin stated

"We may not have a definition but we recognise the children".[4]

The session was drawing to a close and the questioners were beginning to repeat themselves, they would have liked to ask the panel individual questions but of course time restraints precluded this. The closure of the centre was touched on again and it appeared from the transcript that the Inner London Education Authority agreed to set up a diagnostic and teaching centre at Ebury Road, Victoria. However, a questioner felt there was some confusion and, although advertisements had been placed and full-time staff appointed, had the ILEA changed its policy? If it had, why and what could be done, would the ICAA set up a pressure group to establish a centre under the ILEA? In answer, Mrs Bradshaw said the new centre was to be used for in-service training of teachers, and for special courses. She stated that there was a diagnostic centre at present. The builders were in and it was hoped that the centre would be up and running at the beginning of the next academic year. The author has been unable to discover if this centre did materialise. However, much did grow out of the Word Blind Centre as will be seen.

---

4.   White Franklin, "Dyslexia Where Now?", 1972.

In summing-up Sir George Haynes said he had followed the proceedings with interest and he thought that real progress had been made into the understanding of dyslexia. He praised the work of the ICAA harking back to the original conference of 1961, and the resulting interest in the subject that had encouraged the ICAA to continue. He thanked Alfred White Franklin, Sandhya Naidoo and the two funding organizations. The latter had allowed the centre to operate longer than had originally been agreed. He was sure the centre had made a difference and that the ICAA would continue to be involved if only to share experiences.

Sir George understood that dyslexia was a complex problem which required early diagnosis and that the cause should be pursued with psychologists and educationalists in agreement, without which there was less likelihood of progress although he hastened to add there had been a lot of movement on all fronts in the last few years. There was now recognition by the public and the media as seen in the then recent Chronic Sick and Disabled Bill. The dyslexia movement needed to be firm and clear as there was a national call on funds and unless they were they would miss out. Haynes had thought, originally, that there were few dyslexic children, but he now understood they were about two per cent of the population and this number could not be ignored.

The conference saw the end of the Word Blind Centre.

CHAPTER NINE

What Happened Next?

By now most of the characters in this story had moved on. The build-ings were returned to the Hospital for Sick Children. The bulletin was handed on to the North Kent Dyslexia Association. The research was written up and published. The children continued with their education, having in the main benefited from the experience and some teachers and educational psychologist had changed their attitude to a particular groups of non-readers. The work of the Word Blind Centre was like a pebble thrown into a pond, slowly but surely the ripples spread.

Sandyha Naidoo went to work for the National Children's Bureau with Kellmer Pringle who was their director. She was also involved in setting up parents' groups and the Dyslexia Institute. Naidoo developed work with pre-school children and designed questionnaires for nursery nurses. She saw language as vitally important and reasoned that they needed training in this area and as a result of this work it was suggested that Naidoo apply for a job at Dawn House with language delayed children. She felt she wasn't qualified but applied and ended up running a new school on the outskirts of Nottingham where she stayed until she retired.

Macdonald Critchley and Alfred White Franklin continued with their work to the end of their lives. Critchley wrote biographies of the two neurologists who had influenced him most: Sir William Gowers and John Hughlings Jackson, the latter co-authored with his wife, Eileen, and the book was completed just before he died suddenly at home in 1997. White Franklin, like Critchley, continued with his writing.

The teachers at the Word Blind Centre were expected to help run courses for teachers and Gill Cotterell at first found this scary but later came to enjoy it. There were courses in the holidays and at the weekends and they were always full. On leaving the centre she went to Bury St Edmunds as head of educational guidance. There she worked in all the schools in her district and actively looked for dyslexia, although this was not her remit. She also worked with and helped all children with reading problems and aimed to have each at the age of nine with a reading age of 7.5 years. Cotterell tried to identify problems early and had an active rapport with her teachers. She ran courses in the evenings. In 1974, she was awarded the Senior Page Travelling Scholarship from the English Speaking Union and travelled all over the USA where she attempted to meet as many people from the dyslexia movement as she could, including Gillingham and Stillman.[1] There followed a fairly "dull ten years" but at the end of this time she went to the Institute of Education and became an associate, where she worked with Professor Widell. Writing up their work was a mammoth task and she was quite relieved to retire to Suffolk where she did some work but was also able to write the report on her research. She became an assessor for the Royal Society of Arts Post-graduate Diploma course run by Violet Brand and assessed all over the country, though latterly staying closer to home.

Violet Brand was also a teacher at the Word Blind Centre and she set up the first RSA teachers' course to support dyslexics. Maisie Holt went to live on the Isle of Wight, and Bevè Hornsby took over from her at Bart's. Holt appears to have simply retired, her personal autobiography finishes with her years at the centre.

Tim Miles and his wife Elaine continued to work in North Wales, he at Bangor and she as a teacher. Although Miles was the academic he always saw his work with Elaine as a partnership and in designing the Bangor Dyslexia Test she was as important as him. After his work at the centre they began to feel that there should be a special test that just checked for dyslexia, previously tests and assessments looked at reading levels or IQ but did not look specifically for dyslexia.

On observing how children use all the little pauses, questions and fidgets to give themselves time to think of an answer, Miles felt that these

---

1.   Cotterell stayed with local families and during her visit attended a conference at the Mayo Institute where she met up with Tim Miles. They went off to see some geese together, as Tim was a keen bird watcher.

interjections should be taken into account. He was exact in his research, no doubt as a result of his work with Zangwill and Bowlby, and felt that it was important to note these quirks and indicators systematically. From this he and Elaine devolved the Bangor Test.

Tim was proud of the fact that he did not do any experiments for ten years, but listened to parents, and did some teaching "getting to know, getting the feel". He followed the advice of Zangwill "to go in and get the feel of it to see what it [is] like". During this time Miles and Elaine were working out the questions that needed to be used and asked, and refining the interjections into a scalable, scorable test.[2] *The Bangor Dyslexia Test* was published in 1982 and *Pattern of Difficulties,* the book that grew out of the test, in 1983. *On Helping the Dyslexic Child*, a concise explanation of dyslexia and how to start working with a dyslexic child, had been the product of the centre committee, as was *The Dyslexic Child* by Critchley and *Specific Dyslexia* by Naidoo. Miles was made the first Professor of Psychology at Bangor in 1963 and retired in 1987.

The 1961 conference had thrown up the idea for parents' associations. In 1968 a group of parents, including Kathleen Hickey and Bevè Hornsby formed the North Surrey Dyslexia Society. Other local associations sprang up as the Word Blind Centre closed down. Many of the early groups were near London, such as those in Oxford in 1971 and Merton in 1972. Others with obvious links to the centre like the Cheshire and North Wales Association also opened in 1972. Mrs Lilian Harley was responsible for this association, a part-time remedial teacher her aims were to provide professional diagnosis, information for parents and the public and a forum for discussion. Gloucestershire began in 1971, Hereford and Worcestershire 1976 (which may too have had connections); and Suffolk in 1981 was probably encouraged by Cotterell. The furthest flung association appears to have been the Dyslexia Association of Ireland founded in 1972.

After these early societies came about another group following the Education Acts in the early 1980s, South East Surrey 1980, Croydon 1981, South Cumbria 1981, North Staffordshire 1981, West Berkshire

---

2. The answers to the test that were obviously dyslexic were scored with a+ the answers that were obviously not scored with a– and anything in between with an 0.

1983, Ealing 1984 and Leeds and Bradford 1987. By far the most important association was the national group the British Dyslexia Association (BDA) and the founder was one of those "ordinary parents" Marion Welchman. It was formed in 1972 and based in Reading. Tim Miles had a lot to say about Welchman, he remembered her with great warmth. She was his "mother from Bath" who had been disparaged at the 1961 conference but became an important pioneer in the dyslexia movement. Maisie Holt spoke jokingly of Marion because of her background as a midwife, but Critchley on the other hand saw her value. Miles said she was such a tactful person and where others would "go at it like a bull in a china shop she would prefer the old oil", "she did a super job ask anyone".[3] Marion must have heard of the original "committee" and travelled from Bath to meet the members. She was taken to their "caravan" in Coram's Fields and introduced rather snootily: "Here is a mother from Bath who thinks she may be able to do something". This became a standing joke between Marion and Miles who met her on this first occasion. Later when signing her contribution to *Dyslexia Matters* she signed herself "The mother from Bath".[4] Welchman's son was dyslexic and was caned for not being able to spell the word "done"; this inspired Marion to start helping other dyslexic children.

The BDA began work immediately and in 1973 was having meetings with the Department of Education. In 1974 it gave evidence to the Warnock Committee. The philosopher Mary Warnock, according to Miles, was the one to get it right in the report.[5] Elaine and Tim were at college with Mary and Miles was full of praise for he: "She has a brilliant intellect". The Warnock report did not look for a definition of dyslexia but decided on recognition of "special educational needs". By doing this the establishment recognised that the dyslexic needed help and deftly avoided controversy. Nineteen-seventy-seven saw the BDA having formal connections with the Department of Education and Science, however in 1980

---

3. Words in quotes taken from transcripts of interviews by the author with those mentioned.
4. Gerald Hales (ed.), *Dyslexia Matters: A Celebratory Contributed Volume to Honour Professor T R Miles*, 1994, London: Whurr, p. vi. Interview One, 22nd April 2002. Interview Two, August 27th 2002, University of North Wales Bangor, T Miles and J Beard.
5. Mary Warnock, *Special Educational Needs (Report of the Committee of the Enquiry into the Education of Handicapped Children and Young People)*, 1978, London: HMSO.

the British Medical Association advised its members that "dyslexia" was not a medical condition. The 1981 Education Act allowed for children with specific learning difficulties to be statemented and this came into force on the 1st April 1983.[6]

The Word Blind Centre was never a state run unit although local authorities used the facility. The centre's committee hoped a dedicated research and teaching centre would be set up to continue their research and to advise dyslexics, parents of dyslexics and professionals but this did not happen. However, several teaching centres grew out of the centre and research continued in some universities. The teaching centres did as the Word Blind Centre had done and taught the teachers and children and although admirable these centres were all charities and charged fees which placed the teaching out of the reach of a lot of children. Teaching the teachers overcame this problem to an extent as many of the teachers taught were from the state sector and passed on what they had learnt to children in their care. Some of the organizations awarded scholarships to part pay for children's lessons and teacher's course fees.

Helen Arkell had always taught dyslexic children in her area and she also taught some children in London. In 1971, just as the centre was clos-ing, she started her first centre in Crondace Road, London, and it soon came the Arkell Centre in Arkell Lane, Frensham, which grew through-out the 1970s and is still operating. The Arkell Centre began teaching the teachers as well as children and the Royal Society of Arts recognised the qualification offered.

Bevè Hornsby founded the Hornsby International Dyslexia Centre and wrote *Alpha to Omega* in 1975 in conjunction with Frula Shear. It is a step-by-step teaching programme for dyslexics or as the book states anyone having problems with learning to read English. The authors acknowledged their debt to American educationalists: Orton, Gilling-ham, Stillman and Childs, and also to Edith Norrie. However *Alpha to Omega* was also born out of the authors' own clinical experience.

Tim Miles started teaching dyslexic children "who turned up", and initially he shared this with a local teacher, but by the time their son was

---

6. Special learning difficulties became the compromise name for dyslexia. For statementing see *Chapter One*.

seven or eight-years-old he was sharing the work with Elaine. Then they had to start to teach the teachers. They produced an informal qualification called "Language Therapy" which meant the teachers had satisfied Miles and Elaine. They often met at the Miles' home, eight-to-ten people at a time and "basically we learnt from each other". Elaine designed a teaching-programme *The Bangor Teaching System*.[7] Out of this and the research being carried out at Bangor grew the now famous Dyslexia Unit.[8]

The Dyslexia Institute went on to be called Dyslexia Action and dated back to 1968 when a group of parents, including Kathleen Hickey, Sandhya Naidoo and Bevè Hornsby set up a working party which included Wendy Fisher, with the aim of establishing such a body. In 1972 the Dyslexia Institute was founded with Hickey as director of studies and Fisher as executive director. Kathleen Hickey went from the UK in the 1930s to the USA to see the Orton-Gillingham methods in practice and was trained by them in these. She developed a programme during the early-1970s and it was first published as the Kathleen Hickey Language Kit. The Hickey method was formal and structured the teaching sessions, these being short with lots of over-learning and game playing. It attempted to never let a child fail. The programme, basically a phonic method, came in for criticism for being too rigid. There was some falling out between the different groups over the interpretation of multi-sensory which was the cornerstone of the Word Blind Centre's teaching. However, by 1981, the institute had acquired 12 centres nationwide where they taught children and later adults and trained teachers.

All of the centres organized educational psychologist assessments based on the work of Sandhya Naidoo and the Word Blind Centre team. These assessments became important as they were recognised by the LEAs and needed for children to receive extra help within schools, both state and private. Perhaps even more importantly, most universities also required assessments to allow special provision at examinations.

---

7.   Elaine Miles, *The Bangor Teaching System*, 1992, London: Whurr.
8.   Interview One, 22nd April 2002, University of North Wales, Bangor, J Beard and T Miles. In 1986 Miles and Dorothy Gilroy wrote *Dyslexia at College* a book close to my heart as it was one of the first I read on the subject when starting to work at the University of Buckingham. See now third edition by Liz Du Pré, Dorothy Gilroy and Tim Miles, 2007, Routledge.

The Word Blind Centre may not have been directly responsible for the increased interest in colleges of education teaching "reading", this sounds ridiculous but as previously noted it was thought children just learnt to read with no effort on the part of the teacher. Since the end of the Second World War there was a lot more emphasis on teaching children to read but one of the reasons behind the still poor literacy figures was the dearth of teachers who understood the mechanics of reading. This was why teachers were seeking out the courses put on by the dyslexia movement. In the early 1970s this began to change.

In 1970 Reading University ran a course called *Teaching of Reading at Reading* (which of course became an in-joke). Dr Donald Moyle set up a diploma in the teaching of reading at Edge Hill College of Education (ratified by Liverpool University) in 1972. One of the first courses run by the Open University[9] was *Reading Tomorrow and Today 1972.* The introduction to the course reader bemoans the fact that the editors have had to draw on American academics for most of the material, though Joyce Morris features heavily at the end of Part I. Morris, ironically in her article *Phonicsphobia (1994),* praises the dyslexic movement having derided them in the 1960–70s:

"Fortunately, Bevè Hornsby and others working in the dyslexia field have not been unduly influenced by these developments if at all. They have remained steadfast in using and advocating systematic phonic teaching and multi-sensory techniques to help children build a sound foundation for literacy."[10]

Hinshelwood was disparaging of the lack of help for ordinary dyslexic children and suggested anyone could teach them especially their parents who obviously wanted the best for their children. Keda and Harry Cowling have followed in Hinshelwood's shoes and produced, over 25 years, a teaching manual *Toe by Toe* that can be used by anyone who can read, even if not very well. Their argument being that teaching the teacher-reader reinforces their own reading skills so both parties improve. *Toe*

---

9.   The Open University started in 1969 and admitted its first students in 1971.
10.   Joyce M Morris, "Phonicsphobia" 1993 from the proceedings of the Literacy Conference.

by Toe is quite a large tome but the "would be reader" is taken through it in tiny steps hence the title and like all the other programmes mentioned relies on repetition and encouragement to build up the "would be reader's" skills. It is also a favoured method for one-to-one peer mentoring in prisons among other places.

CHAPTER TEN

In Conclusion

It has probably been noted that I have a close personal interest in dyslexia. I was in my 40s before I raked-up the courage to be assessed to see if I was myself dyslexic. I had been working in the field for years and of course knew I was but for one reason and another needed an educational psychologist's diagnosis, and it was confirmed that I am dyslexic, I fall into one of the two groups talked of by the Word Blind Centre, the one that can read but never learnt to spell accurately. After the assessment, I was surprised at how angry I felt, not with the educational psychologist, just angry and it took several weeks for me to stop feeling the anger. I am still not sure why I felt this way but I think maybe it was "if only" syndrome.

When I started school in 1952 there were 60 children in my class. The school was so stretched that the reception class was taught in the local church hall. The classes did not get much smaller, 50 plus being the norm. I don't remember much about those primary years. I drifted through them in a "pea soup" the name given to the dreadful smog of that era.

I remember some kindly teachers, being seated at the front of the class, writing two essays that were praised, one describing my career of choice which was to be a farmer, and another about attending the Royal Show with my brother who was a trainee vet. How the teachers managed to read these essays is beyond me but they must have persevered. I learnt to be good and helpful and I could talk the talk. I do remember taking the eleven plus, I don't know if we had any practice runs but I don't think so. I sat for the length of the test trying to answer one question, I was given the number eight and asked to spell the word "eight" and I couldn't. I failed.[1] The next September I found myself in the playground of a fairly new secondary modern school and I was to go into the third form of a five stream intake, and I knew I was in the wrong stream. I set to work and moved to the top stream in two years and was top of the class. Three things had happened: I had grasped reading and the classes were smaller, in the 30s, I think, and I was determined.

My parents and I moved to the south coast at this point and the secondary modern there was good, supportive and educationally advanced. I managed to get into a teacher training college and the rest as they say is history. The college filled in gaps that I had not learnt at school, for example arithmetic. Learning how to teach basic maths to infants is a wonderful way of gaining the foundations of the subject. My college, Whitelands, was quite advanced. I don't remember being taught anything about dyslexia, but we did learn about reading. Sybil Marshall made a big impression on me. The most important and binding ethos was that each child learns in his or her own way and it is the teacher's responsibility to find that way. This of course is what Gill Cotterell and her colleagues were doing and preaching at the centre.

I eventually came into the dyslexia world like many people before me because of my son. My Percy. Peter was an active child. I can't really remember when he couldn't talk and we thought his odd words amusing, as was his ability to fall downstairs frequently. He had an answer for everything and started school being able to write his name, count up to ten, he knew his colours and could dress himself, all things his reception class teacher was pleased about. When he got to six-and-a-half we realised he was slipping behind his cohort in reading and writing. The same reception class teacher wasn't good so we blamed her for his lack of progress, but things didn't change with the next teacher. The head assured us we were just being over-anxious. At this point a friend with a dyslexic daughter stepped in and told us to stop messing about: "He falls over every time I see him," she said and so he was assessed and was dyslexic.

We looked at our families, on his father's side his nephew and niece are dyslexic and possibly his sister; on my side many of my nephews and

---

1. I told my brother what had happened and he taught me how to take exams. I have never failed one since.

great nephews are and possibly my brother and definitely my mother. This evidence alone should have made us look twice at our own children, but both girls, his older sisters, were fine and so one becomes complacent.

Peter received help in school and we drip fed it at home, he did not want extra tuition from me or from others and we felt he was stretched enough coping with school. His educational psychologist explained to him that he would have a smaller vocabulary because of his slow reading so that he should make up for this by listening to story tapes which he did with a vengeance. He also loved films and would watch them over and over again, I asked him why and he told me first time for the story and second and subsequent viewings for the language. This stood him in good stead as he is now a documentary maker. Prior to this he went to university and achieved an upper-second class degree.

The difference between my son and me is that we knew about his "interesting" brain, I didn't know about mine. The first time I identified my difference was on reading Bevè Hornsby's *Overcoming Dyslexia*. It made me cry. Not for Peter but for myself, all those weird things I did to remember things were not the same for everyone, they were a by-product of my odd brain.

It is difficult to describe one's own dyslexia because it is the norm for that person. There are things that I find really difficult, for example I have never learnt a foreign language. I think the initial grasp of literacy was hard and when I did attempt to learn French I was thrown back into the "pea soup". I suspect that if I had been in the position of spending time in a foreign country I may well have picked up some language. In struggling to learn what I did I probably missed out on a lot, purely because I couldn't read, with ease, Dickens or the Greek myths. Today as a child I would have made up for this with audio books, films ad the internet. Radio 4 has been a great help as has the television and way back Enid Blyton.

The plus to being dyslexic was that it has helped me in some areas of my life. The educational psychologist who tested Peter, David McLoughlin, suggested that as I was a teacher I should go on a course to teach dyslexics, not necessarily to teach Peter but to understand him better. This I did and spent 15 years helping dyslexic undergraduates from around the world to pass their exams. I understood how my dyslexic students felt and they knew this so they trusted me. Luckily I realised early in my dyslexic career that all dyslexics are different to each other and adopted a wide range of learning techniques, and of course the students taught me as well.

Following this story of dyslexia, and to a lesser degree the progress of education in England, has been a fascinating journey. The lessons I have learnt are that the earlier a non-reader is picked-up the less painful is the process of teaching him or her to read and write. This applies to any non-reader, but more especially to dyslexics as they are often capable in other areas of learning and if left they become despondent. This is manifested in numerous ways but being difficult and unhappy are two areas which not only affect the child but also those around him or her. It is also such a waste for children with minor to medium dyslexic problems who if they are not picked out and helped never really catch up and therefore do not reach their potential.

The old class issue rears its head here. Peter was diagnosed privately and because of this we were able to get extra help for him in the state school he went to and eventually he was "statemented". Without the funds for the assessment, or the knowledge we had, none of this would have happened. Hopefully 25 years on things have changed but I suspect this is not the case and it may be things are even worse.

It is moderately easy with a few specific teaching sessions to help children who from the age of six show minor symptoms of dyslexia and this can make a huge difference. It is necessary to also keep a close eye on the child and young person throughout their school life with especial emphasis on A-level and further education years. Dealing with those with mild problems leaves the authorities with more educational funding to help those with severe problems like those seen at the Word Blind Centre.

A big lesson I learnt, I suspect from my siblings, who were all a lot older than me, is that you can't take yourself too seriously. If you muddle your words or forget something just turn it into a joke, most folks would rather laugh with you.

Fashion stalks the history of education as seen in the last century-and-a-quarter covered by this story. I suspect that all natural teachers, those wonderful people with a feel for it, have always used all the tools at their disposal and ignored the trend. No one method of teaching children suits all, be it "look and say" the initial teaching alphabet, real books, or speed phonics. Some children just learn to read, others have to be taught, and those unusual ones have to be helped to find their pathway through the jungle.

CHAPTER ELEVEN

One More Thing

A friend, on reading the original manuscript for this book, said you have talked endlessly about dyslexia but you don't mention how to cope with it. Having agreed this might be a good idea I find I am asking 'What are dyslexics coping with?' As you will have read in the book the ins-and-outs of dyslexia are complicated and tend to cause arguments but I think all would agree that literacy is only one small element that dyslexics have to cope with.

Firstly, it is so important to remember that all dyslexics are different. One with good auditory skills is usually good at answering questions and can fish ideas out of the air; ask them to write the information down and they sit pondering for ages and may come up with a scruffy half page of notes. Another who has good visual skills may not be able to answer questions with ease but can spell quite well. So the number one coping strategy is to know your's, or your child's, or your student's strengths and to use them to bolster the weaknesses.

So what is the problem? What is all the fuss about? Simplistically it is all about the short-term or working memory. To input the long-term memory all actions have to go through the working memory and if this was not bad enough the working memory is also used to retrieve information or actions. Some people have large working memories; those are the ones who cram for exams and come out with flying colours without ever really understanding the questions. Dyslexics can't do this as they have less than efficient working memories. To cope with this problem they have to learn to use what working memory they have as effectively as possible and to download some actions to an automatic memory. Most dyslexics learn to do this over time.

The joy for a teacher of the dyslexic is being able to impart coping strategies to a young child so that he or she has weapons to be used in the battle of learning. So from a practical point of view coping with the working memory is the dyslexic's main difficulty and it is important therefore not to overload it. Most actions use sequences, from putting clothes on in the correct order to sorting out a group of letters to spell a word. One trick to assist the working memory is to learn some things so thoroughly that they become automatic and don't clog up the working memory.

Learning takes place using all the senses. The most obvious ones are sight, hearing and doing (kinaesthetics) and dyslexics are deficient in one or more of these senses, possibly in all three. When an assessment takes place the assessor is able to determine what the mix is and the teacher (or individual) can use this information to make best use of the available working memory. We have other senses as well; smell, imagination, humour and we employ these as well to remember stuff.

Automatic memory is when you always do the same thing time after time, over and over again and your brain knows what to do without thinking. Much of driving a car falls into this category; have you ever "come too" after driving perfectly safely for miles but not being aware of what you were doing? When you automatically carry out an action you don't use much of your working memory, so the more of these tasks you teach yourself or your child the better. One unfortunate aspect of the working memory is that you use it to cope with being distressed; this might be after a bout of "flu" or a more serious, perhaps emotional, breakdown. It also works overtime in new situations, so going to a new school, fresh place of work or even on holiday may be distressing. Skills that have been learnt can disappear temporarily and this can be scary. I hope the following ideas may help a bit whether you be parent or learner.

Pre-school

There are many checklists now available on the internet (for example at understood.org and bdadyslexia.org.uk) if you suspect your child is dyslexic before he or she starts school. Although we didn't know Peter was dyslexic, here are some of the things we noticed about him (and he was the third child, so we'd had a bit of practice):

- He was clumsy, quite dexterous but generally clumsy.
- He used interesting words, sometimes it was missing a letter "nail" for "snail", sometimes a correct word but odd in context, and he carried on saying some blends like the "f" sounds instead of "th" for longer than normal.
- He found learning to ride a bike difficult.
- Telling the time, understanding yesterday and tomorrow, these were all mentioned by Critchley but are still relevant today.

Here are a few general ideas (helpful for any child):

- Dyslexic children find it difficult to carry lots of tasks in their head at one time, so never ask them to do a string of things, two or three maximum. *Please go and get me a nappy for baby sister, thank you, now please will you nip and get her cream.*
- Sing songs and nursery rhymes with actions.
- Talk all the time, when shopping, cooking, watching the television or working on a PC.
- Use all the child's senses, they will naturally learn to use multi-sensory learning methods to fill in the gaps.

If a pattern builds up by the time a child is in school for a year and if it hasn't been picked up by their overworked teacher you may have to be brave and step in. Always talk to the school first but be persistent, some children grow out of minor difficulties but many don't and the longer you wait the worse it is for your child.

Coping strategies for school starters

- Make the school aware if you know your child is dyslexic.
- Your child will be tired, very tired, when they come home and need to recuperate in their own way. As always this will

depend on the individual child, it may be they need to run around a lot to let off steam, or it may be they need to flop down in front of a screen.

- If you have a dyslexic that needs to rehearse what they have learnt in the day give them time to tell all. You don't really need to listen as long as you are supportive. You can make the dinner or go together to walk the dog.
- As the child gets older, homework will appear and have to be done but that may be for negotiation with the school (see the next point below).
- The classroom and the home are always two different places for any child but for the dyslexic child it is so important to be aware of the distinction. School for the dyslexic is hard work, especially for little children, not only are they using the working memory to learn but they are also using it to cope with a new social situation. When the child comes home they will be tired and it is unfair to make them undertake a lot of academic work as soon as they get home. A good homework time needs to be negotiated with the child and it may be necessary to work with the child and the school to make the study time useful
- I don't think children should be subjected to extra tuition. Most schools give extra help to those with learning problems and it is more important at home to bolster their learning through complimentary activities. This could be listening to audio books to make up for not being able to read at their natural level, or going to museums to experience what is being taught at school. However the help is delivered, it needs to be fun and never a punishment.
- Remember you are the parent not the teacher.

Practical day-to-day help

- Lists of one form or another are a good "crutch". Depending on the mixture of strengths. For example, for the young child, colour-coded lists on the fridge door of things to remember for school. A list could be cartoon drawings. The main problem with lists is that they need to be consulted, but at least that is only one thing to remember. Making the list is sometimes enough.

- Whatever the learning task "little and often" is always best.
- Schools in the main don't like fussy parents but sometimes you will have to fight a battle for your child and remember, as Tim Miles always said, you know your child best.
- Reminders, alarms on phones and so on are wonderful for older children and for parents of younger ones. Parents have a lot to remember and maybe are also dyslexic so repeat reminders are a great help. A nudge too for the child to get into the habit of remembering, e.g. their PE kit, homework, the letter from school that sits in the bottom of their school bag.

Coping strategies for the older learner

As your dyslexic child gets older the differences manifested in the younger child will still be there but the individual will have learnt some ways around problems. This, of course, is a good thing but sometimes safe learning skills are not efficient and may need to be adapted.

- Ask the learner how they remember best (if they have a psychological assessment this will be obvious) and then build around it.
- If they learn through images, make plans — "mindmaps" are a great help. If they learn by listening, rehearsing a subject with a friend will help. Equally, swapping over and talking about the plan and rationalising why it has been made will build up strengths and help with weaknesses.
- Study books are full of great stuff but the dyslexic needs to be picky about what techniques they use. It takes most dyslexics a long while to learn something and helpful ideas sometimes just make the task impossible. A student informed me that

although it was great to have a recorded lecture as a backup he just didn't have time to listen to the lecture again. As reading, or rather speed of reading, is usually a problem, asking a friend or family member to read up on the study skill and pass on the information would be a better and more efficient way of getting help. With a bit of searching there are YouTube clips that might fit the bill.

- Planning is essential. Facing up to what is to be achieved and then making longer-term goals and finally planning and executing the short-term tasks.
- Being realistic is difficult but undertaking the minimum but to a good level is probably better than trying to do everything.

My personal coping strategies

- Undertaking a task as soon as I remember it, or making a note if I really can't do it there and then.
- Teaching myself not to butt into a conversation even if it means forgetting an important fact, people who butt in are so annoying.
- Leaving reminders in obvious places to trigger my memory, filing is great but in my experience as soon as something is filed away it is forgotten.
- Tidying-up is good and you find all the things you should have done.
- Laughing at my own mistakes, muddled words have my family in fits of laughter.
- Forgiving myself for what I can't do.

Peter's coping strategies[1]

We started this story with Percy, so I am finishing it with Peter. Here is his own list of how to cope:

- I dispensed with everything I couldn't do.
- The biggest thing I did was find a professional niche that amplified the benefits of dyslexia and made the negatives less important.

More specifically:

- I don't take notes at the point of a conversation and if I do I stop the conversation to make them. "Let me just write down that name".
- I try to understand/question and retain at the time and then make notes about what I felt was important afterwards.
- I never send out an important written communication without it being checked by others.
- I constantly discus everything with my work colleagues — an idea shared means it doesn't have to live in my short-term memory.
- I use alarms to remind me when and where to do things.
- I understand and embrace the fact that some tasks will take me a lot longer than your average Joe. Accept that and find time in your day for it. I try to do my emails at 8 am or 8 pm. At each end of the day when I have time to think.

Most of this stuff isn't conscious anymore.

Good luck.

---

1. Peter Beard, email, May 2015. Peter went to Sussex University and whilst there started to make documentaries. Since then he has worked his way up from a runner to being a director and now co-owns a production company, Story Films. He has made a lot of documentaries and is a two times BAFTA winner. Not bad!

Index

H

I

J

K

L

labelling *113*

language

language delayed children *185*

"Language Therapy" *190*

late developers *66, 70*

laterality *96, 147, 165, 167*

laziness *150, 163*

learning

"learning through play" *58*

multisensory learning *201*

over-learning *190*

Leeds *188*

left-handedness *55, 81*

lettre bâtarde *15*

libraries *24*

lending libraries *24*

Public Libraries Act 1850 *35*

life skills *22*

lists *202*

literacy *16–20, 23, 35, 59, 88, 108, 156, 164, 175, 199*

World Literacy Day *170*

local education authority *64, 133*

London *45, 67, 189*

London County Council *114*

London Jew's Free School *29*

London School Board *31, 32*

"look and say" *47, 60, 97, 197*

M

Macmeeken, Margaret *53–54*

madness *107–116*

magazines *24*

Man Alive *174*

Margaret, Princess *75, 132, 137*

Marshall, Sybil *61, 62, 194*

Mary, Princess (later Queen Mary) *109*

Mason, Charlotte *48, 77*

maturation *152*

maturational lag *148, 170*

McLoughlin, David *195*

meaning *17, 53*

media *86, 87, 115, 150, 174*

memory

automatic memory *200*

kinaesthetic memory *48*

short-term/working memory *199–200*

visual memory *12*

mental health *36, 58, 66–67, 167*. See also *brain*

"low mental capacity" *54*

Mental Deficiency Act 1913 *114*

Meredith, Patrick *90*

Merton *187*

Miles, Elaine *79, 186*

Miles, Tim *69, 78, 98, 110, 129, 140, 186, 189*

mindmaps *203*

mirror

mirror image *148*

mirror writing *56, 165*

monasteries *15*

Montessori, Maria *39, 62, 170*

Moor House School *75*

morality *25, 28*

moral corruption *21*

Morgan, Dr Pringle *11*

"morons" *53*

Morris, Joyce *32, 175, 191*